MIKE STEPH|

STEVO'S
SUPER LEAGUE
DIARY

WITH A FOREWORD BY EDDIE HEMMINGS

impress
SPORT LIMITED

First published in Great Britain in 2004 by
IMPRESS SPORT LIMITED
Fountain Chambers
Fountain Street
Halifax
HX1 1LW

ISBN 0-9547884-2-7

A catalogue record for this book is available from the British Library.

Edited and designed by Tony Hannan.
All pictures Dave Williams at www.rlphotos.com & Sky Sports publicity.

GAMEPLAN

Eddie & Stevo tuck into some pre-match nosh

FOREWORD

BY THE LONG-SUFFERING EDDIE HEMMINGS

"STEVO's writing a diary," they said. "About Super League in 2004!"

"Good God," was my response. "I didn't know he COULD write, never mind remember where he's been week by week over the past nine months!"

"Never mind all that - can you write the foreword?" was the question they continued to ask. Well, of course I can. I'm delighted to be invited to appear on page five of Stevo's Super League Diary!

And what a season it has been for us two personally, as well as the men that really matter - the players and coaches who gave us another memorable year.

Leeds versus St Helens on 23 July 2004 was our 500th Super League commentary together and they say that no other commentators in the big wide world of rugby league have ever done more.

Can you believe that there were actually people around in the earlier days who said that we wouldn't last? And, you know, had I shot him 14 years ago I would probably have been out of jail and a free man by now.

Ah well, let's face it, rugby league would never have been the same.

Stevo and I have enjoyed a rollercoaster of a ride and it's been a pleasure to be sitting there alongside him all these years.

He is a big personality with a huge heart. He'll help out any charitable cause that comes his way and despite the fact that he hung his boots up almost 30 years ago, I doubt if there is a better known face in the game. And he's my mate!

This book will tell you some of the stories behind the scenes at Sky Sports - I hope he treads carefully! I wish him well with it.

Just think, if I hadn't rung him up in Australia in 1990 and asked him to come over and work with me on the Kangaroo Tour of that year, all this might never have happened.

Then we would never have laughed at such phrases as: "Adrian Morley hit him with all the force of an EXERCISE missile!"

Enjoy the book - and here's to the next 500 games!

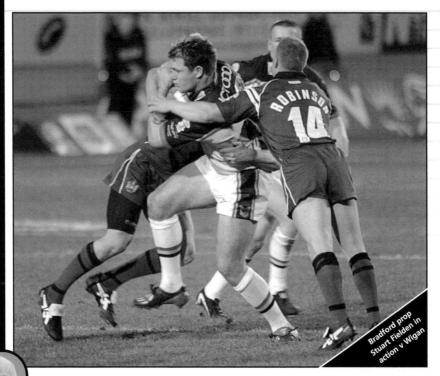

Bradford prop Stuart Fielden in action v Wigan

Elementary, my dear Eduardo!

THE dust had hardly settled at Huddersfield's McAlpine stadium the week before the opening round of Super League and the fans were asking: "who will stop Bradford winning everything yet again?"

Penrith Panthers tried bravely to stop the rampaging Bulls but after the first ten minutes you felt the Aussie NRL champions were going to go home empty-handed and that is exactly what they did.

So with the season hardly even begun there was yet another trophy on the Odsal sideboard and after they put away Wigan in round one, the Bookies were slashing odds right, left and centre and claiming that Bradford were unstoppa-Bull! So, that was that then.

Wigan walloped by the 'Bullies', the Panthers sent back down under with their tails between their legs... it was all over. Let's just give Bradford all the trophies now and call it a day, eh? Brian Noble, the Bulls coach, wasn't getting excited. "There's a long way to go, lots of things can happen during a long season," he said. Smart man. He knows what cruel twists the game of rugby league can bring.

The start of any new season brings its share of nerves and excitement for players and fans alike.

TV star Nell McAndrew helped kick the season off at Odsal

7

Lesley Vainikolo! The Volcano erupted with five tries v Wigan on opening night at Odsal

Stevo's Zero!

Whoever forged all those tickets at Warrington - causing opening night mayhem at the HJS!

Stevo's pearl

"London are going to win plenty of games." - Leeds coach Tony Smith

Rd 1 results

Bulls 34	....	Warrors 6
Giants 26	....	Tigers 22
Rhinos 58	......	Broncos 14
Reds 24	....	Vikings 12
Saints 30	....	Hull 16
Wolves 34	....	Wildcats 20

Even yours truly was shaking like a leaf only hours before Super League IX got underway. That wasn't so much to do with nerves, more the fact it was freezing at Odsal. Thermal underwear was donned by Eddie and myself as we entered the fray.

Yet again, the fans were in good voice with a little rude banter that makes me chuckle and the odd reference to Eddie's hair. Thankfully, he's opted to keep last year's Will Young style and his normal jet black colouring!

Cold it was, but it didn't take long before things got warm thanks to "The Volcano" erupting with such force. Big Lesley Vainikolo was sensational and left a trail of destruction that earned him five tries. I knew the Kiwi international was big and strong but he displayed amazing pace that stunned Wigan to the core.

Bradford looked awesome. They ripped the Warriors apart with some clinical rugby skills and raw power that had the huge crowd begging for more. Many feel Bradford might struggle in Super League IX seeing as how they have lost playmaker Jimmy Lowes, together with hard grafters Mike Forshaw and Daniel Gartner. On opening night, with Robbie Paul and Paul Deacon still injured, Wigan must have thought they were in with a chance.

Wigan had their problems too, though. There was no Andy Farrell, Mick Cassidy or Adrian Lam so they, too, felt understrength. It could have been different if the Warriors had taken their early chances. Danny Orr, Luke Robinson and Kris Radlinski all breached the Bulls' defence but poor finishing let them down.

Bradford didn't look like a side in trouble to me. Karl Pratt was in sensational form and laid the platform for his side's attack but it was left winger Vainikolo who really set Odsal alight.

I had tears in my eyes when Jimmy Lowes hung up his boots after the Super League VIII Grand Final in 2003. I would miss him and no doubt the refs felt the same way, but you can't keep a good man down. As well as joining Bradford's coaching team, Lowes has been given the water carrier's job for this season and he made just as big an impact by having the odd word or two, not only to his own players but also the officials - especially the touch judges.

Who says we don't have characters in our game?

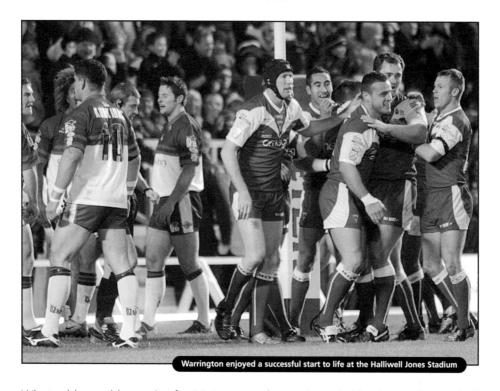

Warrington enjoyed a successful start to life at the Halliwell Jones Stadium

What odds would you give for Mr Lowes to be reprimanded by the Rugby Football League at some stage during this season?

Wigan didn't play too badly, it's just that Bradford were stronger and faster on the night, especially their cover defence which got back quickly for the full 80 minutes. With such an easy win, the fans gave Eddie and me a gentle time as we walked from the Sky Sports studio. Even the jazz band left us alone. Normally, they play the theme tune from "The Muppets", when those two old codgers, Statler and Waldorf, barrack from the theatre box. Peace at last.

The Odsal faithful were full of praise with some suggesting Brian Noble should be given an MBE and Bulls chairman Chris Caisley an OBE. One Super League coach confided in Eddie that the rest were just playing for second spot.

Noble, Caisley and the club are not silly enough to believe the hype at such an early stage, though. They are too professional to do that.

Wigan coach Mike Gregory was a disapointed man after the match, yet his youngsters tried hard and gave him 100 per cent although they will be a much better outfit when Farrell and Lam come back.

With a big crowd at Odsal, we expected the same when we arrived at Warrington's new ground - the Halliwell Jones Stadium - the following day. Wakefield Trinity Wildcats were the visitors and from the buzz being created by the crowd three hours before kick-off we knew something special was on! The Wolves opened their new stadium with pomp, glory, balloons and a huge cock-up! While coach Paul Cullen's charges were striving to get over their visitors' line, some supporters were working just as hard to get inside the ground!

There was talk of over 2000 being locked out, many of them already having bought tickets. The club claim it was nowhere near such a figure. Either way lots of irate fans were less than pleased. Plenty tried to scale the walls via our TV cables! Thankfully, no-one got hurt and who says our game is not worth watching?

The Wolves looked good in the first half. There was some fine open play that confused the Wildcats no end. Although Wakefield produced a spirited fightback in the second stanza, the home side deserved the win. Cullen brushed aside claims that his boys had played poorly in the second half, saying: "A win's a win. A lot of pressure was on the team tonight. Who cares how we got the two points?" He's right.

After the match, Eddie invited me into one of the new corporate boxes owned by a golfing mate of his. It was a nice view but shame about the inside. Bare walls hardly add to the ambience, do they? No doubt this box didn't come cheap, so the least they could have done is smarten it up with pictures on the walls. It felt like being in a prison cell. Only the wine saved the day. I know it's early days but the club need to address it pretty quickly.

I came away from the ground thinking that both these sides would create more than their share of problems for the other Super League clubs this season. Neither of them will be a pushover and both will miss the relegation dogfight.

Sadly that can't be said for Salford and Widnes. Even before the kick-off, Eddie asked me how I could classify a round one game as a four-pointer. Easy, Eduardo. These two are odds-on for the wooden spoon scrap. Salford came out victors and left the Widnes fans somewhat troubled. So much so that rumours already began circulating suggesting that coach Neil Kelly was on his way out. It wouldn't be the first time a club has panicked, but not so soon surely? Kelly has broad shoulders, yet plenty of Super League fans held their breath. Would he make it to round two?

Yet again London had a slow start - does the long off-season abroad (this year three months in Dubai) really work? Leeds just ripped them apart. New coach Tony Smith had decided to give the young half-back pairing Rob Burrow and Danny McGuire their chance from the start and it worked a treat. Who knows, Mr Smith could help Great Britain win the Tri-Nations at the season's end.

Great Britain have struggled to find a solid pairing at six and seven for years. Could this be the answer? The way Burrow and McGuire skipped through the Broncos' defence, it could be "yes".

Hull went to St Helens and took so many fans with them that they delayed the kick-off to get them inside. Wise move but a sad trip as it turned out for the Black and Whites. Saints have recruited well, especially in the forwards. Nick Fozzard and Keith Mason provided the grunt to get the backs moving and Hull had no answer. Hull boss Shaun McRae knew his team had been beaten by a much better team on the night. Ian Millward showed a big grin. His boys looked good. What's all this talk of Bradford winning everything?

Millward's former assistant and new Huddersfield coach Jon Sharp was another happy chappie. A solid performance in beating Castleford lifted the Giants and the spirit of their fans. Huddersfield have so often struggled to crack the big time. If they play like they did against the Tigers, who knows?

Once again, another great start to Super League. Wonderful games, bumper crowds, the race for Old Trafford and the Super League IX Grand Final is on!

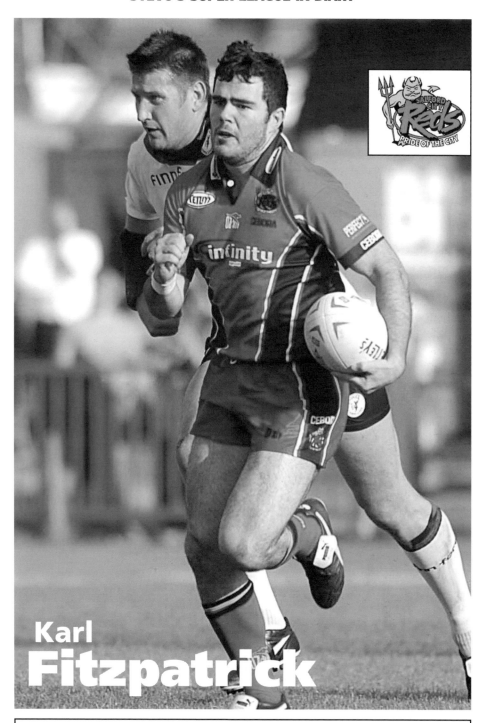

Karl
Fitzpatrick

AUTOGRAPH

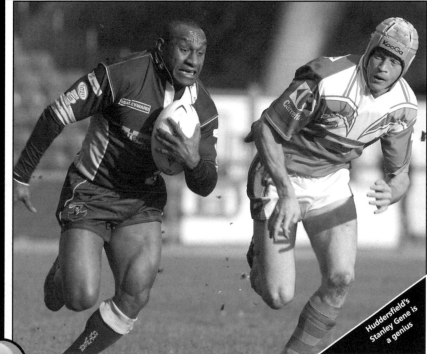

Huddersfield's Stanley Gene is a genius

One Giant Step for Stan-kind

IT'S not a dream. Huddersfield are top of the Super League table courtesy of a convincing win over Widnes.

Okay, the fact that they beat the Vikings in a Friday night match did give the Giants a head start on everybody else, but they are up in the clouds on merit. No doubt the big clubs won't need Jack and the Beanstalk to drag the big fellow back down, but come Saturday morning Jon Sharp and his boys were basking in the glory after beating a Widnes side that was woeful to say the least.

Huddersfield showed enough to suggest that they have to be in with a chance of a crack at the play-offs this year. In the likes of Stanley Gene, Paul Reilly, Brandon Costin and Paul March they have a solid foundation to build upon.

It isn't easy for Sharp to follow in the footsteps of Tony Smith; a coach who instilled toughness in defence and an ability to squeeze out tries in his team. So far this season, Huddersfield have shown more flair. They still tackle with that rugged style, especially March, their hooker-cum-half-back. This guy would beat a ravaging dog to a bone that has been tossed into a corner and, no doubt, push his own mother out of the way in the process.

Not that they had to break into a huge sweat to put Widnes away. Far from it. And the crowd were quick to get on the Vikings' back with plenty of shouting for coach Neil Kelly's head.

The fans were seething. They could see quite easily that flair, effort and skill

Danny McGuire. The Leeds dynamo scored a hat-trick against Cas in front of a record crowd at the Jungle

Stevo's Zero!

After 7 months out, Hull forward Richard Fletcher's comeback ended with a broken leg after just 12 minutes

Stevo's pearl

"You can't blame the coach if the players let him down" - Widnes chairman Tony Chambers

Rd 2 results

Tigers 8 ....Rhinos 34
Hull 24............Wolves 18
Broncos 12 ......Saints 26
Wildcats 6 ....Bulls 40
Vikings 6..........Giants 38
Warriors 20 ....Reds 10

were all at a low level. Most of all their team looked unfit. The display did nothing to convince Mr Kelly he would be staying at the Halton Stadium, especially when the club's chairman publicly apologised for the team's poor showing.

A fit-looking Stanley Gene proved a huge thorn in the Widnes defence. To think this guy was supposed to be all washed up and past his best. Yet I struggle to think of another player who can get the crowd buzzing everytime he gets the ball quite like Stanley can. Go, Stanley! Go! Go! Go!

After this poor effort Widnes became favourites to go down. There's a long way to go, I know, but they look devoid of ideas and their defence

Referees controller Stuart Cummings was on the phone

is a shambles. Even the fans thought so. I had a few beers with them after the game and got swamped. One fan suggested that I take up coaching again. I know Widnes were bad but surely not that bad for the old fellow to get out the tracksuit.

It's amazing to think that Neil Kelly was coach of the year not so very long ago in 2002. Now they want rid of him, although he did get the dreaded vote of confidence from the board who must take some of the blame. Any club who can afford to let the likes of Phil Cantillon leave is asking for trouble. All coaches, players and board members should take a good look at themselves in the mirror. As for fitness, maybe the Atkins diet could help!

I got a call from the RFL's director of referees Stuart Cummings. He wants to meet up and discuss the new interpretation of the rules. That's fine by me as

STEVO'S SUPER LEAGUE IX DIARY
ROUND TWO

long as he does the same to the referees. Once again the merry whistle-blowers create pain for myself, players and fans alike. It's a tough job but they are the ones who choose to do it.

Despite having injury problems, a cock-a-hoop St Helens went south to London after their great win over Bradford Bulls in the Challenge Cup. Not surprisingly, Ian Millward inflicted another of his famous last-minute changes on us!

The media had been reporting all week that Sean Long was nowhere near fit. Guess what? He played after all. As it happened, Long and his teammates hardly broke sweat against a Broncos side that produced probably their worst showing in a first half since the club began. They bucked their ideas up in the second half but, by then, the game was

Salford boss Karl Harrison watched his team go down to Wigan

won for Saints. Tony Rea was fuming afterwards and wisely let the players stew in the sheds rather than give them a blast. That was to come at training. His side played even worse against Wakefield in the Challenge Cup.

Bradford's gloom at being knocked off the road to Cardiff by Saints was lifted somewhat by their Super League win over Wakefield but the bitter taste was still there. The Rhinos went on their merry way with a great win at Castleford where a huge crowd witnessed some scintilating open play from both sides but more from Leeds in the end. Once again, the Burrow-McGuire combination took the headlines in Yorkshire.

Wigan bounced back from their opening night loss at Odsal by downing a spirited Salford at home, yet Reds coach Karl Harrison was pleased that his side held in there and gave Wigan plenty to think about. The question was still being asked, though: "Would Salford be able to handle the fitness levels and pace of their Super League rivals?" Despite the loss, Harrison is eager to get at Wakefield on home soil in round three, in what will again be a four-pointer!

Wigan's Stephen Wild

Saint Nick Fozzard

14

Chev Walker goes on the rampage

Headingley in the clouds

THE dark clouds were gathering at Headingley after St Helens once again dumped a top club out of the Challenge Cup.

This time their victims were Leeds Rhinos and Tony Smith's boys were chomping at the bit to entertain Wigan at the start of round three. Leeds boss Smith changed a few positions, dropping winger Mark Calderwood, bringing back Francis Cummins and allowing Andrew Dunemann to partner Danny McGuire, with Rob Burrow on the bench. More stability was needed and so was a good kicking game, something which had been lacking against Saints. Wigan were missing key players Adrian Lam and Andy Farrell but they still fielded a strong outfit. You just knew it was going to be a classic and, boy, they didn't let us down.

The ball handling and support play were sensational. They produced some great tries, especially the one scored by McGuire, who ran 70 diagonal metres with five players handling the ball in the build-up. All that to a roar from an 18,000-plus crowd that would have knocked over a donkey.

Yet it was the kicking game that proved the difference. Full credit to coach Smith, who had insisted on plenty of hours at training perfecting the short and long kicks. That time proved well spent when the first of Leeds' tries came from the boot. Rhinos skipper Kevin Sinfield was having the time of his life. It was good to see him back to his best form. I thought the captaincy would affect his open individual performance and last year, a few times, it did. Tonight, all that was pushed to one

Stephen Myler. The youngster had a wow of a game at scrum-half for Widnes at Knowsley Rd

Stevo's Zero!

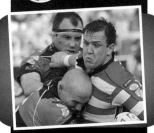

Wigan's Danny Sculthorpe felled Leeds full-back Richard Mathers with an outrageous off-the-ball high-shot

Stevo's pearl

"There's one or two people sharpening their knives"
- Cas coach Graham Steadman

Rd 3 results

Giants 6..............Bulls 20
Hull 46 ....Broncos 4
Rhinos 36.....Warriors 24
Reds 20 ....Wildcats 27
Saints 38........Vikings 20
Wolves 32........Tigers 18
Re-arranged Rd 17 match
Broncos 35 ....Reds 30
(played 20 March)

side as he plotted and directed the show. Mind you, one factor remains missing. Leeds still lack the killer instinct. They get the opposition on the ropes and can't throw the finishing blow. Sinfield reckons they will eventually. Time will tell.

One thing is for sure, though. Leeds have a star in full-back Richard Mathers. This guy glides across the turf, has great balance and a keen eye for an opening. We will see a lot more of him.

To be fair to Wigan, they never gave in and found more than a few holes in the Leeds defence. Yet again, though, poor support play or a bad pass let them down. One thing coach Mike Gregory has to do is calm some of his players down. They give away too many silly penalties. Danny Sculthorpe is one who lost the plot tonight. He should have got more than just a warning for a bad late tackle on a player off the ball.

Yours truly went the same way when Wigan's Martin Aspinwall was awarded a late consolation try by the video ref. It was clear to anyone that he failed to get the ball down with controlled pressure. He finished with both palms on the whitewash and the ball still up in the air. No way should that have been given. Thankfully, the result didn't depend on it but try telling that to the poor punters who have a bet each week on the spreads!

Saturday saw us back with the Sky Sports cameras at Salford, a treat we had missed whilst the City Reds were playing in National League One. They make us welcome at the Willows and always put on a jazz band. Sadly, though, the ground hasn't changed much since I played there and hopefully their new stadium will be built soon. They need it to lift their spirits. Without being too unkind, their defence was shocking.

Why it often takes a good bollocking by the coach at half-time to get things going baffles me. Karl Harrison certainly gave them some words of wisdom and they produced a much better second 40. But Wakefield had breached them so easily early that they always looked confident of getting the spoils.

Salford looked like a division one side and they will need to improve or they will be back down again come September. Only their hooker Malcolm Alker showed anything like top-quality form. Wakefield, on the other hand, once again showed toughness, flair and some wonderful team spirit. It was that which got

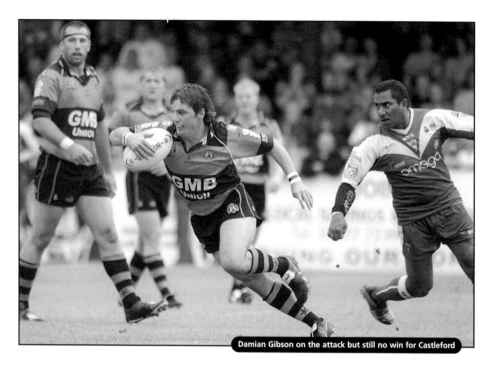

Damian Gibson on the attack but still no win for Castleford

them through. The Wildcats, like Huddersfield, could be the shock performers this year. Both teams have similar playing styles and, of course, a March in each side snapping at the heels of the opposition. Wakefield also have a good half-back pairing in Ben Jeffries and Jamie Rooney and a stylish player in Gareth Ellis. That, coupled with a strong pack, will test any team this season.

Widnes, buoyed by the vote of confidence for their coach, put up a great display away at St Helens. The Vikings bossed the show early to take a well-deserved lead and it took some magic from Sean Long to steer Saints to victory.

The Giants came down to earth against Bradford, who had Robbie Paul back in a bruising encounter. The Bulls may have lost their grip on the Challenge Cup but they are keen to keep all the other trophies. That won't be easy, especially with new signing Toa Kohe-Love sidelined for the season.

After a wobbly start to the year, Hull thrashed poor old London with the visitors just not in the hunt at the KC Stadium. Pace, skill and effort were missing from the Broncos and things look bleak. Coach Tony Rea is optimistic and says they will bounce back. Jokingly, I suggested to London's owner David Hughes that he might like to ring up that Russian bloke who owns Chelsea FC, telling him to sell his fifth-choice goalkeeper and buy the Broncos, thereby adding to his collection of clubs in London. David was far from impressed.

Nor was Castleford coach Graham Steadman, who thought his struggling side might start to find a winning formula at Warrington. It didn't happen. Paul Cullen's boys are on fire so the Tigers are still looking for their lost roar. Sadly, Ryan Sheridan will also miss three months of the season with a bad shoulder injury. The Wolves combined well to overcome an eager Castleford side, with Danny Lima, Lee Briers and Mike Wainwright all showing up well.

Semi
Tadulala

AUTOGRAPH

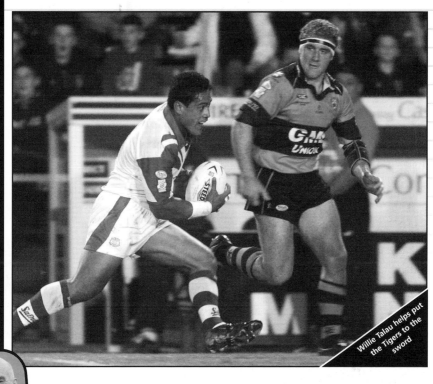

Willie Talau helps put the Tigers to the sword

Rocked Steady's beat

THE mighty St Helens machine rolled into Castleford full of confidence after yet another gruelling Challenge Cup tie that saw them beat Hull in a thriller.

The Tigers still hadn't won a game but coach Graham Steadman felt sure the fortnight's rest would help his boys to give Ian Millward's team a run for their money. It did. A little more steadiness and discipline and Castleford could have turned their visitors over.

Rumours suggesting that Steadman could be sacked were rife. The club had given him the dreaded "vote of confidence" and even the most ardent Tigers fan couldn't see him being their coach for much longer. Steadman himself was upbeat due to the fact that his troops had at least played the full 80 minutes for the first time this season. Ryan Hudson once again put his heart and soul into proceedings but he must keep control over his emotions. His discipline was poor in the first half and gave Saints the green light to control the game. Despite tiring late in the match, St Helens held on thanks to a supreme effort from Jason Hooper. His long-range try and assist early in the second half gave his teammates enough of a margin to hang on.

St Helens are on a roll. They look super fit and confident with a pack that works hard throughout. Nick Fozzard and Keith Mason are proving to be shrewd buys with their crash-bang tactics creating the ideal springboard for the likes of Sean Long, Paul Sculthorpe, Willie Talau and Paul Wellens. The spread of their

Stevo's Hero!

Cliff Beverley. The tricky Salford half-back scored a hat-trick against Bradford Bulls

Stevo's Zero!

The April Fool prankster who put out a "press release" saying that Warrington had signed Iestyn Harris

Stevo's pearl

"Castleford won't run last"
- St Helens coach Ian Millward

Rd 4 results

Bulls 25...............Reds 18
Tigers 14 ....Saints 22
Giants 26 .....Warriors 10
Broncos 24 .....Wolves 36
Wildcats 21 ....Hull 27
Vikings 0 ....Rhinos 46

workload is second to none. It's going to take a good team to stop them on this form and that's probably why their away support is so good.

Saints fans are vocal to say the least. They give me some stick and at one point refused to go away after the game. That made it a nightmare for Eddie and myself to wrap up the game on Sky. Thankfully, the microphones can't pick up most of what they sing, although I should point out that they are totally wrong about my sexual preferences. I don't have a closet, never mind coming out of one!

It proved to be a night for hanging on. Salford went to Odsal with fire and brimstone blazing in their bellies and three tries from Aussie Cliff Beverley almost provided one of the biggest upsets in Super League history. Leading 18-10 early in the second stanza, the Reds looked in control. The Bulls had made several clean breaks but their final touch was letting them down.

Salford's great start to the game forced Bradford coach Brian Noble into sending on substitute Robbie Paul. Paul's arrival improved his team but the Reds just wouldn't lie down until Lesley Vainikolo's late try saved the Bulls from embarrassment.

Neil Kelly's position as Widnes coach continued to be under threat

So much for those pundits who predicted that Bradford would race away with all the silverwear yet again! Karl Harrison was full of praise for his side and underlined the fact that there would be no easy games for anyone this year.

Once again Wigan struggled to overcome injuries to star players yet nobody expected them to be taken to the cleaners by Huddersfield, who are going to be knocking on the door come play-off time.

Jon Sharp has done a great job and was all smiles with the 26-10 win over the Warriors. No longer do people laugh at the Giants - especially when

Brandon Costin and Stanley Gene get going. Both were outstanding but were overshadowed by full-back Paul Reilly.

Reilly is all class when he concentrates on playing open rugby rather than getting excited and wanting to bash everything that moves. Sharp has changed both Reilly's attitude and that of his entire side. No longer are they just bang and bash merchants, they are playing some outstanding rugby league. Wigan had no answer to Huddersfield's new style of play and the Giants go into their Challenge Cup semi-final against St Helens with more than faint hope.

Beaten quarter-finalists Wakefield and Hull trotted out at Belle Vue in wet conditions yet gave us all a treat. Boy, was this a tough one! Nobody took any prisoners and with several fights breaking out, referee Ronnie Laughton had a busy night. Darrell Griffin and Richie Barnett senior went to the sin bin, the latter losing heavilly on points with blood streaming down his face. It always amazes me when a threequarter takes on a prop forward!

Once again a poor refereeing decision - or in this case a failure to take action - probably stopped Wakefield from at least snatching a draw. Trinity skipper

	P	W	D	L	Diff	PTS
Rhinos	4	4	0	0	128	8
Bulls	4	4	0	0	83	8
Saints	4	4	0	0	54	8
Hull FC	4	3	0	1	40	6
Giants	4	3	0	1	38	6
Wolves	4	3	0	1	34	6
City Reds	5	1	0	4	-17	2
Warriors	4	1	0	3	-46	2
Wildcats	4	1	0	3	-47	2
Broncos	5	1	0	4	-107	2
Tigers	4	0	0	4	-52	0
Vikings	4	0	0	4	-108	0

TETLEY'S SUPER LEAGUE AT MON 5 APRIL

Gareth Ellis had his leg nearly twisted off and was then pushed to the ground directly under the Hull posts. Referee Laughton ignored pleas for a penalty which was confusing, seeing as how he had warned Hull twice in the last 15 minutes for messing about at the play-the-ball. A penalty would have given the Wildcats a chance to earn the draw they deserved. That would have been a fair result and rewarded both sides for putting on a great show in such lousy conditions.

Hooker Matt Diskin was the star of the show as Leeds thrashed poor Widnes, who look likely to be in the running for the wooden spoon and relegation. Joining them in that battle will be London, who failed to overcome Warrington in the capital.

Yet again both clubs claim their coaches Neil Kelly and Tony Rea are not under threat. Maybe so, but I bet neither will be sleeping well.

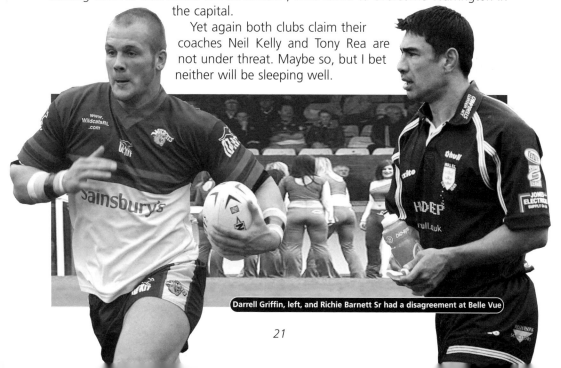

Darrell Griffin, left, and Richie Barnett Sr had a disagreement at Belle Vue

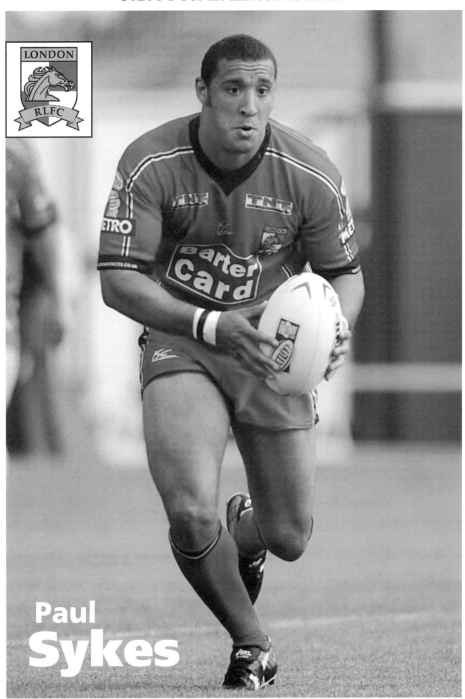

Paul Sykes

AUTOGRAPH

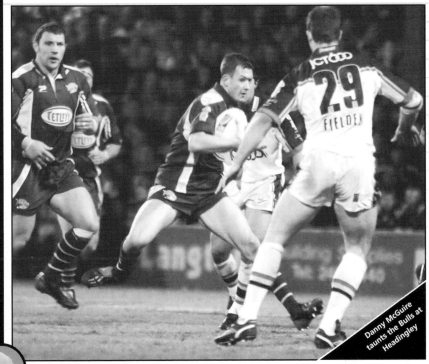

Danny McGuire taunts the Bulls at Headingley

Revenge of the Rhinos

THE build-up to Easter could not have been better with Leeds and Bradford putting on a classic in front of a full house at Headingley. Despite losing five times to the Bulls last season, the Rhinos were confident of revenge and got it big time!

Plenty of Leeds fans asked me the same question as I walked across the car park towards the Sky Sports TV gantry: "Could Leeds do it?" "Yes," I replied, a fact confirmed by the welcome from the South Stand fanatics.

Those delightful words "Stevo, sumo, Stevo, sumo" were ringing in my ears as I trod my way lightly over the exposed gantry bridge. This time, though, they were sang well and with more gusto. Tonight the combined voice of the Southstanders sounded and felt different. It was a more confident style of abuse. You could have cut the atmosphere with a knife.

It wasn't bad on the pitch either! Both sides went at each other like men possessed - there were no prisoners tonight! It was a game that would have done justice to a Grand Final. The speed was unbelievable and the handling skills superb on what was a very chilly evening.

It was also a night on which we may have seen the launch of Danny McGuire's Great Britain international career. I have been an admirer of this kid's talent for ages, even suggesting it was wrong to leave him out of last year's third Ashes Test. The series was over and it would have been a great chance for David Waite, the GB coach, to give youth a chance. Sadly, Waite spurned the opportunity

Stevo's Hero!

Danny McGuire. Celebrated his Player of the Month award with a couple of tries against the Bulls

Stevo's Zero!

There were 17 of them in the Warrington team that were shot down by Widnes

Stevo's pearl

"He's not happy unless he's talking" - Wigan boss Mike Gregory on Ian Millward

Rd 5 results

Giants 24............Reds 16
Hull 26................Tigers 4
Rhinos 26 ....Bulls 18
Broncos 16...Wildcats 39
Saints 21 ....Wigan 21
Wolves 16......Vikings 24

but after McGuire's showing against Bradford, he has to be given a chance at the top level.

Ironically, it could be Bradford's coach Brian Noble who will give him the nudge up. Noble is hot favourite to take over the national coaching job and he must have been impressed by the Leeds stand-off's performance.

McGuire proved the difference between the teams although his coach, Tony Smith, raised a few eyebrows by selecting him to start the match from the bench. As it turned out, that was just another coach's ploy to fool the opposition. McGuire started and dominated the game.

Why coaches are prone to play hide and seek with the media and the fans is beyond me. Have they all joined the secret service? Still, if that little bit of fun and games irritated the press, then what was to come on Easter Monday made Tony Smith look like a saint.

Or was it a case of Saints being sinners?

Either way, Leeds deserved the spoils and convinced me that they do have the killer instinct to wrap up the tight games.

It was McGuire's kick that provided Andrew Dunemann with a try, even though Vainikolo replied soon after thanks to a neat inside pass from another player not on the early teamsheet,

Shontayne Hape. The Rhinos always looked in control, though, especially when McGuire ensured Leeds went in ahead at half-time. His superb piece of footwork helped Marcus Bai score four minutes from the break and the Rhinos never looked back.

Bulls coach Brian Noble was still pleased with his side's effort and rightly so. He suggested that both

Chris Joynt comes in for close attention as Saints & Wigan fight out another thriller

these teams would be there or thereabouts come Grand Final time and I agree.

Saints and Wigan would have plenty to say about that comment, of course, and the Good Friday derby proved to be another thriller.

St Helens ripped Wigan apart in the opening 15 minutes, with the Warriors once again looking like a side down on confidence and deserving of their unusual position in the lower half of the Super League table. Then came the rain and with it a change in Wigan's fortunes.

Slowly but surely, with sleeves rolled up, they fought their way back into the game led by Andy Farrell, who took them into the lead with a drop-goal five minutes from time. It looked all over but the cool head of Sean Long snatched another one-pointer on the bell to draw the match. I love a late drop-goal, me, and here I was with two to drool over!

I am not so keen on all-in brawls, though, and the clash was spoiled by one that had players running in from all angles to land punches. Samoan winger Dominic Feaunati was one of the worst culprits and threw punches like a seasoned boxing champ. Not surprisingly the new Saints star was put on report, along with Paul Sculthorpe and Wigan skipper Andy Farrell. Five days later, Feaunati received a three-match ban, Farrell escaped with a £500 fine, allowing him to play in the Challenge Cup semi-final clash with Warrington and Sculthorpe had no case to answer.

The disciplinary committee's decision upset many fans. One sent me an email asking if the Rugby Football League had made new rules saying that any player who runs in from 15 metres (Farrell) gets away lightly whilst anything over that distance (Feaunati - 20 metres) merits a suspension.

That's a good point and it will be interesting to see what happens if another mass brawl breaks out this season. For mine, that's on the cards if referees keep ignoring shady high tackles. Quick action could have prevented these ugly scenes but the merry whistle-blower and his touch judges chose to turn a blind eye to plenty of high tackling in the lead-up to the fight.

Either way, both sets of fans went home damp and cold knowing that their side had deserved a draw. Sadly, nobody was talking about the game, only the brawl.

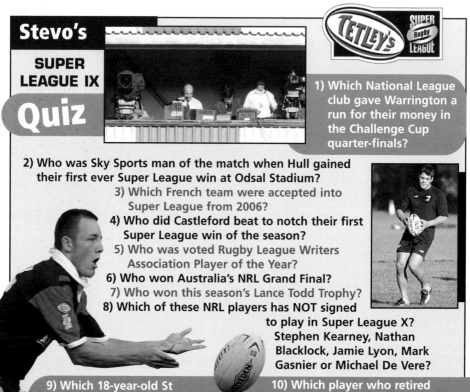

Stevo's SUPER LEAGUE IX Quiz

1) Which National League club gave Warrington a run for their money in the Challenge Cup quarter-finals?

2) Who was Sky Sports man of the match when Hull gained their first ever Super League win at Odsal Stadium?

3) Which French team were accepted into Super League from 2006?

4) Who did Castleford beat to notch their first Super League win of the season?

5) Who was voted Rugby League Writers Association Player of the Year?

6) Who won Australia's NRL Grand Final?

7) Who won this season's Lance Todd Trophy?

8) Which of these NRL players has NOT signed to play in Super League X? Stephen Kearney, Nathan Blacklock, Jamie Lyon, Mark Gasnier or Michael De Vere?

9) Which 18-year-old St Helens prop captained the England Under 18 Academy team to a first ever win on Australian soil?

10) Which player who retired from Super League this season is the record points scorer for both England and Ireland?

ANSWERS on page 98. No peeking or I'll set Eddie on you!

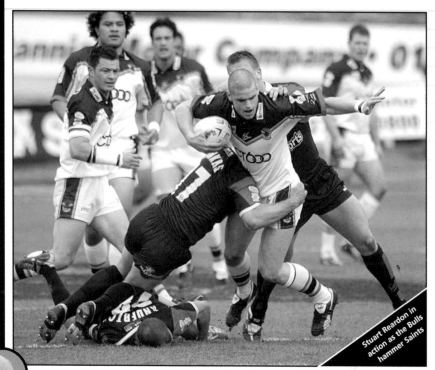

Stuart Reardon in action as the Bulls hammer Saints

Basil's brush with controversy

DRIVING to Bradford on Easter Monday was a breeze. No heavy traffic and a few glimpses of sunshine - what a perfect start to the day.

Little did I know that what was to unfold would send shivers down my spine and fill me with rage.

Any game at Odsal these days is a treat. There's always top entertainment, a real buzz from the fans and a Bulls side full of quallity and class. Today there was also the chance for the Bulls to lock horns with high-flying St Helens.

Mouthwatering, eh? The fans certainly thought so. There were thousands of them at Odsal two hours before kick-off and the Saints faithful were in good spirits after their classic draw with Wigan three days earlier.

What unfolded was beyond belief. At first, three Saints players were deemed unfit. Then it became eight. Then 11. What should have been a terrific match was reduced to a farce and I felt sorry for both sets of fans. When the teams were announced ten minutes before kick-off, there were four players I had never even heard of! One was called Peter Cook. All it needed was Dudley Moore to show up and the comedy would have been complete.

Ian Millward is no stranger to controversy. He did the same thing against Bradford two years previously, ahead of another important Challenge Cup tie. On that day, he even played the latter part of the game with 12 men, refusing to send on another sub to make up the numbers.

Stevo's Hero!

Widnes stand-off Jules O'Neill's superb kicking game earned their second win in two weeks

Stevo's Zero!

St Helens coach Ian Millward's antics at Odsal let the game down big style

Stevo's pearl

"We prepared to fight George Foreman and got George Formby" - Bulls coach Brian Noble

Rd 6 results

Bulls 54 ....Saints 8
Tigers 34 ....Broncos 42
Reds 0 ....Rhinos 44
Wildcats 17 .....Giants 24
Vikings 32 ....Hull 18
Warriors 26 ....Wolves 24

Not surprisingly, Saints got thrashed and it was the same this time around.

Millward was quick to point out that he had only abided by the rules, a fact borne out by the RFL's announcement three days later that neither the coach or his club had done anything wrong.

By the rulebook, maybe. But, since 1895, rugby league has been proud to call itself "the family game". What happened at Odsal was certainly nothing for the sport to be proud of. Try telling the Saints fans who gave up their Bank Holiday to venture over the Pennines and pay hard-earned cash to watch a match that was nothing short of a training run that Millward acted correctly.

In normal curcumstances I would discuss the game. Not this time. No way. It shouldn't even be recorded in the official stats.

The Sky Sports cameras were eager to pick out the "injured" Saints, who looked quite happy with proceedings. Little did we know that a few days later the horrible truth would come out with claims of a betting scam. Apparently, Sean Long and Martin Gleeson had bet on their own team to lose heavily and picked up a bundle of cash for doing so!

This revelation was unknown to fans at the ground, of course. Yet such was the anger from the crowd that hundreds converged on our Sky studios after the match to voice their opinions. So much so that they wouldn't let me pass before discussing this dreadful slur on our game. Many even suggested that I was to blame and most advised that I did something about it.

As it happened, I didn't have to. The media went wild and so did coach Millward in the aftermatch press conference. That turned out to be a tickle on the backside compared to the body blow the game would receive the following week. Everyone was devastated, me included. Bulls coach Brian Noble summed it up neatly: "We prepared for George Foreman and got George Formby instead."

Throw in the fact that Jon Wilkin was sent off for a high challenge on Bradford's Paul Deacon, resulting in a four match ban and £300 fine, and it was a disaster of a day for all concerned.

Talking of devastation, Graham Steadman was once again on the rack as Castleford Tigers played like Castleford Kittens. They lost badly to London Broncos

London's former Castleford star Jon Wells gets a warm welcome back to the Jungle

despite taking an early 10-0 lead at the Jungle. Full credit to London, though, who dragged themselves back into the match with some outstanding kicking from Jim Dymock and thrilling running from Dennis Moran. Broncos boss Tony Rea was more than pleased with his team's effort. The media had long suggested that his job was on the line but it was Steadman's head that the Tigers fans were after.

It's sad, really, seeing Castleford's sorry plight. The club has embraced the Super League concept so well. Yet fans want wins and success. Nothing less will do. Many expected the Tigers coach to go but there was more pain to come.

Richard
Horne

AUTOGRAPH

The Rhinos have made a sparkling start to the season

Long odds on fair coverage

GOT up on Friday morning none too pleased, which was a surprise seeing as how Eddie and I had hosted a charity function in Huddersfield the day before, to help the Giants' new junior campaign.

I had enjoyed every minute of it only to be disgusted this morning by the three-page spread in the *Daily Mail*, featuring messrs Long and Gleeson and the betting scandal.

I know that betting against your own club isn't the right thing to do. It's even worse when you use your own name to open a betting account! All sportsmen have a bet. The thrill of competing in sport is matched by the odd wager. No doubt both these players will pay the price as the season unfolds, yet that wasn't the reason I was mad. When was the last time you saw so much space dedicated to rugby league in the national press?

There were five action shots, the players' records, how much they earn, blah, blah, blah de blah. In the same paper, not one word about the Leeds v Huddersfield match at Headingley! First versus third in the Super League table deserves something at least.

Compare that to the three rugby union stars who sold tickets for a game at Twickers and probably made more profit than Long and Gleeson's pay-out together. At most, I spotted four paragraphs on that disgraceful episode in the press.

When will people in this country realise that our game of rugby league

Stevo's Hero!

Wigan winger Brett Dallas scorched in for a hat-trick as Wigan beat Warrington to reach the Challenge Cup Final

Stevo's Zero!

Sean Long & Martin Gleeson, above, were fingered by the media for their part in a Super League betting scandal

Stevo's pearl

"It was not my bet. I opened the account for my mate" - Sean Long

Rd 7 results

Tigers 10 ......Wildcats 42
Rhinos 38 ....Giants 6
Broncos 34 .....Vikings 18
Saints 40 ....City Reds 4
Postponed: Hull v Wigan, Wolves v Bulls

should not be shunted into the inside pages, alongside table tennis, squash etc? As much as I do not condone what has happened at St Helens, we at least deserve better exposure for the game itself and not just for what happens off the field.

Sadly, like their fellow Challenge Cup semi-finalists Saints, Huddersfield also had problems with injuries. Five of their top players would miss the Leeds showdown so the innuendo got top billing from the fans. Not that the Leeds South Stand faithful cared much either way. A win and topping the Super League table was all they wanted.

This mob, alongside Warrington's fans, are the loudest in the game. Thankfully, the old-style 'Loiners' don't have a drum. Not yet anyway.

To be fair to the Giants, they put in a tough performance and kept Leeds at bay for long periods only to fade badly against a strong Rhinos outfit. Danny McGuire once again showed plenty of class but only late on in the match. Up until then he found playing against Brandon Costin a hard task. Not so his frequent half-back partner Rob Burrow, who came off the bench to create havoc.

I make no excuses for being a fan of "Beep Beep". Never mind Wile E. Coyote, the Roadrunner himself couldn't catch him!

Leeds boss Tony Smith was all smiles afterwards. His team's defence was once again solid and he would have been pleased at how his side have stopped giving away silly penalties - a huge problem last term. The Rhinos are going to take a lot of stopping in this mood. They work hard for each other and are running the angles well. There's a feelgood factor at Headingley these days and only silverware will sate their appetite.

Once again Sky's cameras went to Super League IX's very own "last chance saloon", aka the Jungle. There aren't many smiling faces down the lane these days and coach Graham Steadman looks older each time we see him. That is quite a lot of late. No doubt he would have wanted to shun the TV limelight over the past few weeks.

Stevo's Top 5
Props

1. ANDY FARRELL
   Wigan
2. PAUL KING
   Hull
3. STUART FIELDEN
   Bradford
4. DANNY WARD
   Leeds
5. MICHAEL KORKIDAS
   Wakefield

LEFT: 2004 World Club Challenge winners

CENTRE L to R: Coach Brian Noble takes in water; Stuart Fielden enjoys a telling off from ref Steve Ganson; Odsal's gameday entertainment is hot!

BOTTOM: Lesley Vainikolo on the rampage. INSET: Jamie Peacock leads the Bulls out on Super League IX's opening night at Odsal

CASTLEFORD TIGERS

KINGS OF THE JUNGLE:
Top - Graham Steadman,
Middle - Gary Mercer,
Bottom - Brad Davis

TOP RIGHT: Steven Crouch
wrestles Salford

CENTRE LEFT: Bloodied
Castleford skipper Ryan
Hudson can't bear to look

CENTRE RIGHT: The Tigers
& Leeds players have a
minor disagreement.
GOING DOWN: A parachute
drops into the Jungle

BOTTOM: The Tigers players
& fans are disconsolate as
Castleford's Super League
relegation is confirmed

ABOVE: Phil Joseph keeps his head warm!

LEFT: Darren Fleary finds it heavy going against Widnes

BELOW LEFT: Sean Penkywicz gets away a flamboyant pass.
BOTTOM: Darren Turner takes a breather during the Challenge Cup semi-final defeat to St Helens

BELOW RIGHT: Paul March lines up another conversion attempt for the Giants

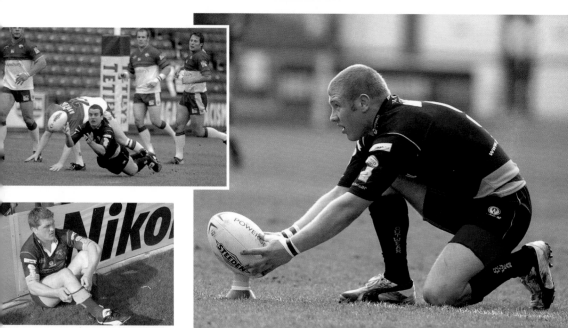

HULL F.C.
Est. 1865

FAR RIGHT: Paul Cooke had a
magnificent season for Hull

RIGHT: Shaun Briscoe showed
Wigan just what talent they had
let go from the JJB Stadium

ABOVE: Paul King was inspirational for Shaun McRae's men all year.
RIGHT: The Hull fans indulge in some light-hearted banter at Headingley
BELOW: Andy Bailey accepts the applause of his team-mates

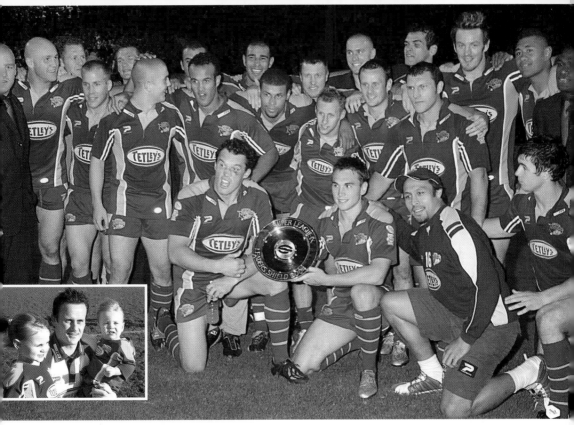

ABOVE: Leeds Rhinos are awarded the League Leaders Shield at Headingley.
INSET: Francis Cummins & family kick off the Leeds favourite's testimonial year

LEFT: Papua New Guinea international winger Marcus Bai terrorised Super League defences all season long

ABOVE: The Cheeky Girls put in a special guest appearance at Headingley.
BELOW: A familiar sight for Rhinos fans in 2004 - Danny McGuire scores a try

RIGHT: Steele Retchless in action against Warrington. The London stalwart retired at the end of Super League IX and has been a loyal servant to the Broncos

BELOW: The Griffin Park Cowgirls have all the fun!

ABOVE: The London players celebrate a crucial victory at Widnes' Halton Community Stadium

RIGHT: Richard Moore runs into some stiff opposition as the Broncos shock high-flying Wigan

FAR RIGHT: Dennis Moran came back to lead London's successful battle against relegation

LEFT: Despite being the best centre in Great Britain, St Helens sold Martin Gleeson to rivals Warrington

BELOW LEFT: Kiwi centre Willie Talau made a massive impression on the Knowsley Road faithful

BELOW: Paul Sculthorpe takes on Huddersfield with Jon Wilkin & Keith Mason in support

LEFT: The talented Jason Hooper was an early contender for the 2004 Man of Steel award

BELOW: An injured John Stankevitch is helped from the field

BELOW RIGHT: Hooker Mickey Higham gives the London defence plenty to think about

SUPER SAINTS: St Helens' wonderful start to the season culminated in a Powergen Challenge Cup Final victory over Wigan at Cardiff's magnificent Millennium Stadium. Alas, it was largely downhill from here...

POWERGEN CHALLENGE CUP

Castleford's Jamie Thackray takes it up but the Wildcats came out on top

Some teams lift their game when they are on television but Castleford look camera shy. This was another one they just had to win, a local derby with Wakefield and what better way to get their season underway? Trinity are no pushovers these days, though, and so it proved.

Again the Tigers held a lead only to let Ben Jeffries scoot in before half-time and set the nerves jangling. When props Michael Korkidas and Darrell Griffin turned in a sensational effort in the second stanza, you knew Castleford were in for another hiding. The two Wildcats forwards impress me each time I see them. They run at the defence with such gusto and are the best demolition company I've witnessed in years. It's good old-fashioned stuff, no frills with plenty of guts. These two fight each other to get to the ball first. They were the highlight of the round and, boy, didn't our game need a lift?

Not that it helped the Jungle mob who realise now that their off-season signings just haven't produced. Sean Rudder in particular, who came with big raps from Australia.

Ironically, the Tigers played better when the stand-off went off injured, leaving Francis Maloney and Jon Hepworth to run the show, both of whom had far more ideas. Even that couldn't prevent Wakefield a deserved victory, though. A number of Castleford fans stayed behind to vent their anger, shouting things that were none too nice about all concerned with the club. Just to give you some idea of how low things can get, some of the fans were chanting for yours truly to take over as coach! With strains of "Stevo's Barmy Army" ringing in my ears, I trudged away from the famous ground thinking it was desperate times indeed.

After that episode the club can surely only go up from here on in.

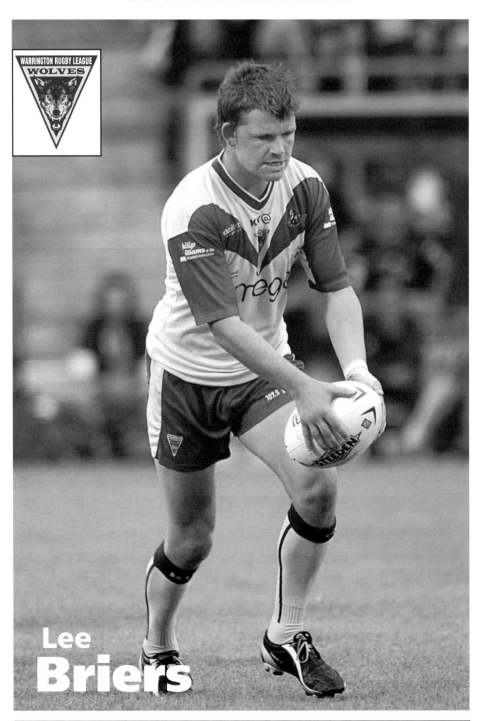

Lee Briers

AUTOGRAPH

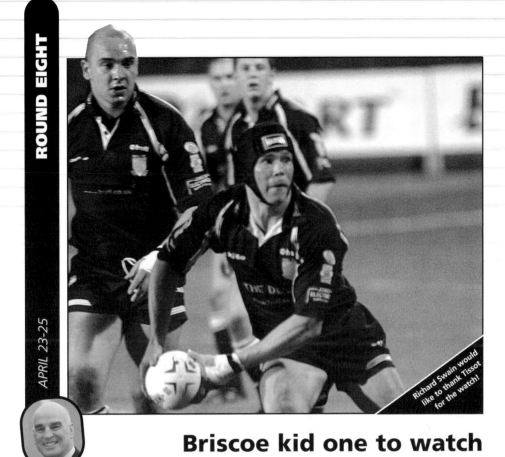

Richard Swain would like to thank Tissot for the watch!

Briscoe kid one to watch

WOULD I tell a lie?

No sir, this was no Bull. Bradford and their coach Brian Noble knew it and blew it! Who could believe it when Hull came back from the dead to overwhelm the home side and inflict yet another defeat on the world club champions? I was stunned and the Odsal crowd were too. It was the quietest I have heard them in years.

The sensational victory over Penrith Panthers to clinch the world title seemed a decade ago. Where is the spirit, fight and controlled football that knocked the Panthers off their stride? Gone, that's for sure. The Bulls had a lethargic look about them and seem lost out on the paddock at times.

After the way Bradford started the season, people had to rethink the idea that the Bulls were going to miss the likes of Daniel Gartner, Mike Forshaw and Jimmy Lowes. The truth now, though, is that they do. That was never more evident than watching the boys from the black and white stuff take them to the cleaners. Hull coach Shaun McRae had been saying for quite some time that his side were capable of pulling one of the big boys down. When four-try hero Shaun Briscoe scooted in for his last four-pointer, the Bulls had been slaughtered big time.

With only minutes to go Briscoe must have been admiring his left wrist and thinking about the Sky Sports man of the match Tissot watch that would soon be wrapped around it. Then media spokesman Dave Hadfield announced that, in fact,

Stevo's Hero!

Shaun Briscoe is still looking for a watch despite scoring four tries against the Bulls

Stevo's Zero!

Struggling coach Graham Steadman was finally shown the door by Castleford

Stevo's pearl

"They were very good" - Huddersfield coach Jon Sharp after his former team St Helens won their Challenge Cup semi-final with ease

Rd 8 results

Bulls 18 .... Hull 26
Reds 18 .... Wolves 37
Wildcats 12 ..... Rhinos 36
Vikings 29 .... Tigers 18
Warriors 64 ..... Broncos 8
Postponed:
Giants v Saints

Richard Swain had won the prize. It would be the former Kiwi international hooker telling the correct time instead of the free-scoring, fiery-haired full-back!

I was quick to point out that ignoring Briscoe's claims to the award was "a brave move". Not brave enough, if the faces on the disgruntled fans who called for the blood of the *Independent* scribe were anything to go by. Welcome to the world of television, Mr Hadfield. No more is the pressure on yours truly to come up with the star of the show and David was soon to find out what a bunch of irate fans can do to your thinking.

To his credit, Hadfield shrugged his shoulders, took the flak and stood by his guns. Swain performed well, especially in the second half, so he was on the right track. Yet I can't remember any player who scored four tries, saved two and hardly put a foot wrong for the full 80 minutes being denied the chance to take the bacon home.

Hours before, New Zealand lost to Australia in the Anzac Test in Newcastle, New South Wales. Bulls boss Brian Noble may have sensed that it wasn't going to be his day when Robbie Paul got injured in the same match and Lesley Vainikolo

Stevo's Top 5
Wingers

1. LESLEY VAINIKOLO
   Bradford
2. MARCUS BAI
   Leeds
3. STUART REARDON
   Bradford
4. BRIAN CARNEY
   Wigan
5. COLIN BEST
   Hull

copped a battering in the face also. Fair play to Noble, though. He didn't put Bradford's loss down to missing such world class performers. Instead, he pointed to a lack of discipline, although he did wonder why his side had suffered so badly in the penalty count. Take nothing away from Hull, they battled on throughout and deserved the win.

It was a tough encounter and I was in need of a drink after the match. It's amazing how the excitement makes you thirsty. I sloped off to have refreshments with Mr Hadfield who looked slightly on edge. "Never mind David, the fans are fickle," I said, trying to comfort the big fellow in his hour of need. "It's not the fans I'm worried about," came the reply. "It's the fellow journalists."

Salford hosted the next Sky game, hoping that the cameras might just help lift them to bigger and better things. Sadly it wasn't to be, despite a huge

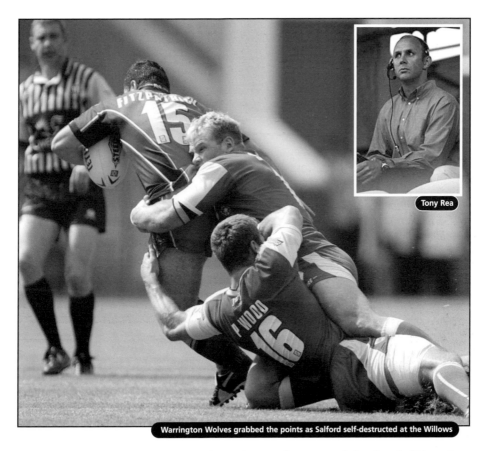

Tony Rea

Warrington Wolves grabbed the points as Salford self-destructed at the Willows

effort on their part. They contained Warrington for most of the first half but then coughed up an intercept to Lee Briers, who raced away the full length of the field to score with only ten seconds left to half-time.

Reds coach Karl Harrison displayed great composure by not breaking the nearest person's neck. Instead, he kicked the water bucket with a lunge that Bruce Lee would have admired. Sadly, Salford faded away late in the game to give the Wolves an easy win in the end.

Despite knowing that they had a big home game against what was sure to be a fired-up Bradford the following Tuesday, Warrington put in the hard yards and showed some tactical prowess. None more so than Briers, who put in a brave effort by playing with a badly-swollen broken finger. He full deserved his man of the match award. These are not good times at the Willows. Salford are trying hard yet lack ideas. Like many clubs, they now feel that some of their off-season buys didn't come with a big bonus bag.

And so to Warrington's new HJ Stadium for the showdown with the Bulls on a wet midweek night. Surely this time the Bulls would get it together against a side with 24 hours less preparation than they had enjoyed and with near-torrential rain making energy levels a vital key to success.

What unfolded will live with me for a long time. Both outfits put on a display worthy of a Grand Final and, boy, did they give it to each other. Especially

Paul Cullen's boys who brushed, banged and sometimes bashed Bradford into what should have been submission.

Many felt the 22-22 draw was a fair result. Try telling that to Mr Cullen, who left us in no doubt that his side had bombed victory by giving away silly penalties late in the game. Those indiscretions gave the Bulls the green light to fight back and that's exactly what they did, thanks in the main to a steal by Stuart Fielden on Briers midway into the second stanza. It's funny how a little thing like that can change the game.

At 18-6 up and after correctly having three close chances turned down by the video referee in the first 40 minutes, Warrington looked to be coasting. Bradford had no answer. Once again, Lee Briers ran the show. His kicking, passing and control of the game was so impressive that you felt he was giving the newly-announced Great Britain coach Brian Noble a huge "hello".

Brian won't need to check his post. Briers made clear his intentions for a spot in Britain's Tri-Nations squad at season's end, although he almost came a cropper in scoring a wonderful solo try by nearly stepping on the dead in-goal line whilst sneaking a look at a spare seat in the stands so he could sit down and applaud himself. Confidence is no problem with Mr Briers! He got the nod from the video ref by a mini-second. Any later and the try would have been turned down.

Our studio guest, London coach Tony Rea, suggested that he should have been shot if the result had been in the negative. Tough game, eh?

Briers was outstanding and so was prop Danny Lima, who my mate Eddie suggests is like the tyro Aussie Les Boyd. He's right is Eduardo. Lima belts them with gusto, although too many high shots and a silly penalty given away late lost him the man of the match award.

Instead, that went to prop Mark Hilton. The groans from the crowd indicated that Mr Hadfield was at it again! I don't call rugby league the greatest game of all for nothing.

TETLEY'S SUPER LEAGUE AT MON 26 APRIL

	P	W	D	L	Diff	PTS
Rhinos	8	8	0	0	236	16
Saints	7	5	1	1	44	11
Bulls	7	5	0	2	113	10
Hull FC	7	5	0	2	56	10
Giants	7	5	0	2	21	10
Wolves	7	4	0	3	43	8
Warriors	7	3	1	3	12	7
Wildcats	8	3	0	5	-23	6
Vikings	8	3	0	5	-91	6
Broncos	9	3	0	6	-162	6
City Reds	9	1	0	8	-124	2
Tigers	8	0	0	8	-125	0

Andy Coley was a key figure in Salford's season but he couldn't prevent defeat to Warrington

London Broncos gave the Bulls a run for their money

Raining champs slip sliding

ANOTHER Bank Holiday and the weather didn't let us down.

It poured with rain and made the London v Bradford match a bit of a lottery. Poor London coach Tony Rea had spent the entire week leading up to the game trying to find players from other clubs, owing to the Broncos' massive injury list.

A full squad would have given the Bulls a run for their money, especially with Brian Noble's boys hardly hitting the high notes. With a scratch side it looked like mission impossible. In the end, Bradford were made to fight all the way by a courageous London team, for whom Dennis Moran showed great leadership quallities. They still couldn't stop Bradford taking the points, though.

Not that the win gave the Bradford board much to be happy about. The Bulls chairman, Chris Caisley, has never been short of a word or two. His face alone showed that things aren't rosy at Odsal just now. Nor would the announcement of Brian Noble as part-time GB coach have sent the outspoken chairman into cartwheels of delight. Brian, I know, will give his heart and soul to both jobs. Maybe when Great Britain lift the Gillette Tri-Nations trophy and Bradford trot away from Old Trafford as champions yet again, Mr Caisley will force a smile.

The acid test for league leaders Leeds was a visit to St Helens; not only a chance to avenge the Challenge Cup loss earlier in the season but also an opportunity to show the rugby league world that Mr Smith and his boys were

Stevo's Hero!

Wakefield hooker David March scored 16 points as Widnes were demolished 40-10

Stevo's Zero!

Salford coach Karl Harrison was "totally embarrassed" by his team's pathetic display at Hull

Stevo's pearl

"They are an outstanding team, aren't they?" Ian Millward's sarcastic appraisal of Leeds Rhinos

Rd 9 results

Tigers 28 ......Warriors 42
Hull 82 ....Reds 6
Saints 56 ....Rhinos 10
Wildcats 40 ....Vikings 10
Wolves 20 ....Giants 26
Broncos 12 ....Bulls 24
Rearranged Rd 7 match
Wolves 22 ....Bulls 22

---

serious contenders for the Super League IX crown.

Little wonder the Rhinos crossed the Pennines confident that they could pick up a victory that would open up a huge gap at the top, leaving them kings of the castle with the other clubs struggling to stay in touch. The motorway was packed with Rhinos fans, so it was no surprise to see Knowsley Road full to the rafters.

The game was always going to be a crunch clash and it had the added spice of a public war of words between the two coaches in the week leading up to it. An outspoken Smith had told the press that the Long and Gleeson betting scandal had done the game an injustice. "Sadly our game has suffered," he claimed. Millward was quick to point out that St Helens had not gone public with their views over the two Leeds players who were given custodial sentences the year before.

It was a nervous night all round and sparks were going to fly, especially when Millward announced before kick-off that Leeds would be no problem. "They are a good side but nothing changes," he said. "They came here last year top of the table on an unbeaten run, but we turned them over. We will do so again."

Fighting words, but the Saints coach was offering no idle boast. After watching how clinically Saints had already taken apart Huddersfield in the Challenge Cup semi-final, everyone knew this was going to be a mighty contest.

The atmosphere was electric and the Saints fans, as usual, were in good voice. They gave Eddie and me some stick as we walked to the gantry. I felt that the locals were restless and itching for a fight but unfortunately they didn't get one. It was all over in minutes. Saints just blew Leeds away, no contest. It all left the Headingley faithful with fears that, once again, they may have been looking at a false dawn.

Mind you, Saints were outstanding. They blasted the Rhinos to bits. Seeing as how Leeds held the best points for and against totals, you could only wonder at how neither their defence or attack ever got going.

We all expected a tough encounter with both sides sparring for the opening 15 minutes, searching each other out, probing for weaknesses, but Tony Smith's boys never got out of the blocks. Trouble was, Leeds looked incapable of probing a cauliflower ear and Super League's best defence collapsed courtesy of Long, Cunningham etc who breezed past their opposition with ease.

It was classic stuff that will have sent a few shivers down the spine of the rest of the teams in the competition. Ian Millward may not be everyone's cup of tea but he sure as hell can coach. The way he has brought out the skill factor in the two props, Nick Fozzard and Keith Mason, is a clear indication that the bloke knows what he's doing. Little wonder that Sean Long is on fire, with these two blokes ripping into the defensive line. Smith conceded that Saints were awesome. "A bad day at the office," was how he described it. More like a shocker!

The St Helens fans

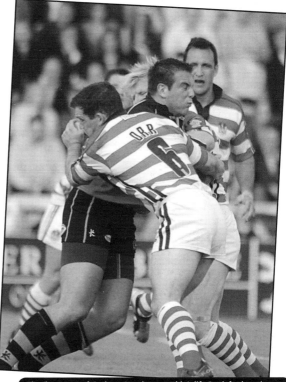

The departure of Graham Steadman couldn't lift Castleford to victory

couldn't give a monkey's. They were over the moon. So much so that many of them offered nice words to yours truly after the game, which is a first. I must be slipping.

Back over in West Yorkshire and with Graham Steadman finally sacked, Castleford's faithful were looking to new stand-in coach Gary Mercer to give them something to cheer about. The players' performance was certainly better and they gave it a good shot against a strong Wigan outfit. Mercer did raise a few eyebrows, though, with his comment that he felt the Tigers were "not fit enough". That was a surprise, seeing as how two weeks ago he was Steadman's assistant. Why didn't he speak out then and perhaps help change the situation?

Wigan still had enough firepower to overcome the eager (and fitter?) Castleford side. Yes, there was improvement but one wonders if that will be enough to give Mercer the job on a full-time basis. The word was that the Jungle bosses were not rushing into things, despite rumours linking John Kear and Neil Kelly with the post. Even Eddie is convinced that Mr Kear will get the nod. He posed the question to Hull boss Shaun McRae about standing in John's way if his assistant coach was approached and Shaun made it clear that, while he didn't want to lose his second-in-command, he wouldn't stop him from taking a senior coaching position.

My guess is that they will appoint someone from down under and that Eddie's brain has been affected by the fumes from his black hair dye. Ah well, time will tell.

Gareth Raynor sizes up the Huddersfield defence

Tadpoles apart in Huddersfield

RAIN, rain and more rain. Where is the sun?

That's the question most fans want answering and who can blame them? Standards have dropped and conditions are not conducive to fancy play. Well done to Huddersfield and Hull for trying, though.

So much water had drenched the McAlpine Stadium - it wasn't called the Galpharm yet - that huge puddles had formed on the outskirts. Even more incredible was that they were full of tadpoles! Yes, tadpoles! I couldn't believe it. Hundreds of them.

But the opening game of round ten was no 'tiddly' matter. Hull knew a win would leapfrog them above Huddersfield into third place on the table. That was a position the Giants were fighting hard to maintain, so the scene was set for a tough encounter.

Sadly, Huddersfield's recent rise to lofty heights has failed to attract the public so yet another disappointing crowd was on show. Why the public at the birthplace of the greatest game of all turn up for soccer yet stay away from rugby league is baffling. Giants boss Ken Davy must be tearing his hair out. Coach Jon Sharp has got his side playing some good stuff and they deserve better.

Those fans who do turn up give it their best shot and make plenty of noise. As did the travelling supporters from Hull who, despite the rain, made the long trip and went home happy. Hull were impressive, especially Paul Cooke and second

Bradford's Stuart Reardon scored four tries as the Bulls sent Castleford to another defeat

Stevo's Zero!

Aussie ref Ashley Klein controversially ruled out a David March try and cost Wakefield victory at Saints

Stevo's pearl

"I'm sure we'll push on well with Brian," - GB captain Andy Farrell welcomes Brian Noble

Rd 10 results

Bulls 44 ....Tigers 18
Giants 0 ....Hull 20
Rhinos 23 ....Wolves 10
Reds 30 ....Broncos 12
Saints 26 .....Wildcats 20
Warriors 26 ......Vikings 8

rower Paul McNicholas who deservedly won the man of the match award.

Hull played solid tactical rugby league football with a good kicking game and chase to match. Shaun McRae has them doing the basics right and his team seems to have shed last year's tag of being injury prone. Like all the other clubs, though, they have yet to put out a consistent starting line-up. When they do they will be strong contenders for Old Trafford. Don't write them off. Forward power, linked with a fast threequarter line, will trouble anyone.

Trouble is the key word when it comes to relegation battles and Saturday's clash, when Salford hosted London, was always going to be a four-pointer. Reds coach Karl Harrison had publicly announced his team's embarrassment for their shocking display at Hull, when they shipped in a disgraceful 80 points.

He's a proud man, Karl. No doubt he said the odd word to his players in the week's build up to this tussle with the boys from the capital. Once again, the Broncos were struggling to fill their squad of 17. A combination of youth and borrowed players was always going to take its toll and, with such a short preparation time having played Bradford the previous Monday, it looked unlikely that London would leave Manchester feeling anything other than disappointment.

I firmly believe that the clubs with most depth will contest the Grand Final and that lighter line-ups will struggle.

London are an example of a side who don't have a lot in reserve. Playing out of a development area makes it harder to compete and they won't get back into top of the table contention without big crowds to boost their finances. The Broncos do a good job with what they have and give everything each week.

Yet the stark fact is that they don't attract the huge crowds needed to make playing in London viable and something has to be done. I have often suggested that they up-stumps and go to Wales, a place where they have played games before with improved crowds. Why not bite the bullet and go to Swansea etc? I know it will upset those faithful few but business is business.

I certainly upset one Broncos couple who gave me a right earful at such a suggestion when I made it on Sky's midweek magazine show, "Boots 'n' All", a few weeks earlier.

Salford man of the match Gavin Clinch took a roasting from coach Karl Harrison

London tried hard but Salford were in no mood to be sentimental. With the kicking of Gavin Clinch giving them the upper hand it was always going to be the City Reds' night. For once, the Salford defence was solid which nearly had Mr Harrison breaking into a smile. I say "nearly" because he wouldn't let our sideline guru, Bill Arthur, into the dressing room to give Clinch his man of the match Tissot watch.

"Man of the match?" he shouted. "With that last kick of the game he doesn't deserve it!" Apparently, Karl was hurt by the fact that Gavin's kick allowed London to score a length of the field try right on the bell. The result was never in doubt but that didn't stop Karl fuming and he gave everyone in his sights a right verbal spray.

Watching Castleford coach Gary Mercer left the Willows knowing full well that the Tigers' next opponents down at the Jungle would be no easybeats. If Castleford are to gain their first Super League win, though, at least they will have two weeks to prepare for it. Then again, so will Salford.

Next week, it's Challenge Cup Final weekend starring St Helens and Wigan in Cardiff. In Super League, things are hotting up at both ends of the table.

Stevo's Top 5
Second Rows

1. DAVID SOLOMONA
   Wakefield
2. ALI LAUITIITI
   Leeds
3. WILLIE POCHING
   Leeds
4. JAMIE PEACOCK
   Bradford
5. LEE GILMOUR
   St Helens

AUTOGRAPH

Castleford called in
Ellery Hanley to help
Gary Mercer

A lovely stick of Ellery

What a shock!

Ellery Hanley to coach the Tigers - didn't that set up the weekend for fireworks? There is no doubting the man's ability. His record is good and he is just the right person to instill a more professional attitude at the club. Hopefully it will change Castleford's fortunes, kick-start their season and maybe even allow the press to get him talking!

Ellery made a quick impact alright, but, it wasn't enough for the Tigers to snatch their first Super League IX points. Salford spoiled the party by winning 36-32. Close but not close enough for the Tigers.

Gary Connolly's return to Wigan was another event that raised a few eyebrows. Leeds had made it clear that he would have to play second fiddle to young Richard Mathers, who again displayed skills aplenty in helping the Rhinos down Hull in a thriller at the KC stadium on Friday night.

What an atmosphere and what a game, especially the first half where the 0-0 scoreline defied logic. Time and again both sides made breaks yet defence and a little bit of panic allowed the scoreboard operator to put his feet up and relax. We didn't. The studio was buzzing and so was the crowd. Wonderful stuff. Leeds threw everything possible at Hull but somehow the Black and Whites held out, although one could see that the effort in defence was always going to make the second half a tough one for Hull.

Stevo's Hero!

Martin Gleeson had a stormer v Warrington, as Challenge Cup winning Saints got back to Super League action

Stevo's Zero!

Poor old Quentin Pongia's playing career was all-but ended when news of his Hepatitis 'B' virus broke

Stevo's pearl

"I want to give something back to the game" - Ellery Hanley, on his arrival at Cas

Rd 11 results

Tigers 32 ....Reds 36
Hull 12 ....Rhinos 23
Broncos 6........Giants 30
Wildcats 14..Warriors 20
Wolves 20 ....Saints 50
Vikings 20 ....Bulls 30

Leeds were outstanding. So were Hull and it took some magic to turn it the Rhinos' way. Mathers, Andrew Dunemann, David Furner, Rob Burrow and Kevin Sinfield all hit their straps against a determined outfit that surely must have its eyes on a top-four spot at least, despite their loss. The game would have graced Old Trafford it was that good.

Although Richard Horne finished up on the losing side he impressed enough to be in the running for Great Britain selection later this year. His strength, determination and upper body strength all combine to make him a special candidate for this autumn's Gillette Tri-Nations. Leeds fullback Mathers should also gain international recognition if he continues to play like this.

On to Saturday and Eddie, the Sky Sports crew and myself were still excited about the Hull-Leeds clash. We felt it would continue at Warrington, who played host to a St Helens side that had been celebrating big time since winning the Challenge Cup in Cardiff seven days before.

Like many others, I thought it would go the way of past years when the Cup winners have traditionally run out of steam in their next Super League fixture. Trouble was, nobody told Saints!

Once again they showed sheer class in taking Warrington apart. Not that the Wolves didn't play well, far from it. St Helens were outstanding. Martin Gleeson and Sean Long showed yet again that off-field distractions over the betting scandal have done little to dent their enthusiasm. Few can live with Saints in this mood and not surprisingly the bookies have made them favourites for Old Trafford.

With a scoreline of 50-20, you might have expected Warrington coach Paul Cullen to be upset. But he felt that his side had made the breaks but failed in execution.

With five losses in seven games, the Wolves fans were getting restless yet even they could see that their team had improved considerably. Mind you, Cullen's gamble with selecting players who weren't

Stevo's Top 5

Full-backs

1. RICHARD MATHERS
   Leeds
2. SHAUN BRISCOE
   Hull
3. PAUL WELLENS
   St Helens
4. KRIS RADLINSKI
   Wigan
5. PAUL REILLY
   Huddersfield

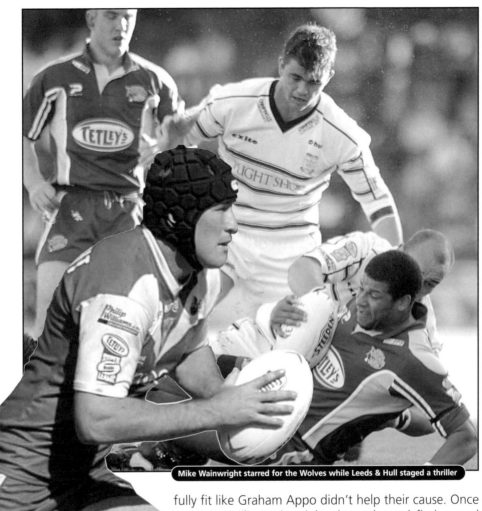

Mike Wainwright starred for the Wolves while Leeds & Hull staged a thriller

fully fit like Graham Appo didn't help their cause. Once again, Mike Wainwright showed good flashes and has been Warrington's most consistent performer so far this season.

Saints coach Ian Millward couldn't praise his side highly enough. "Great effort, I'm very proud of them," he said. And so he should be considering their star hooker Keiron Cunningham had left the battle early. At least that allowed Jon Wilkin a chance to impress, which he did in more ways than one. Saints just keep turning them out!

At Wakefield, the Quentin Pongia Hepatitis 'B' saga was pushed to one side with a tough win for Wigan. London struggled against Huddersfield and Widnes gave the Bulls a surprising run for their money. The relegation struggle for Super League survival is on a knife-edge.

Wigan coach Denis Betts raised eyebrows over Adrian Lam

Lam to the slaughter

DARK clouds, strong winds, drizzle, rain... it must be a Bank Holiday again.

Not that we didn't get any sunshine, well a few hours anyway, but the Super League boys came up trumps yet again and gave us plenty to smile about. Especially Warrington Wolves, who took Wigan apart on a gloomy night in Cheshire.

The game will be remembered for a lot of reasons, none more so than the substitution fiasco with Wigan's Adrian Lam. Stand-in coach Denis Betts dragged off the Papua New Guinea international after 20 minutes. No injury, just poor form is what he told us later. It left everyone stunned, particularly as Lam wasn't even called on to replace Danny Orr when the former Castleford star was carted from the field of play late in the match. Days later, both Betts and Lam declared that they had sorted out whatever dispute they had and that there was no panic at the club. After the way Warrington bashed them, then outplayed them, the alarm bells must be ringing at the JJB stadium.

How long does it take to eat a hot dog? That was the question buzzing around Nathan Wood who, after dummying both Gary Connolly and Kris Radlinski and scoring a sensational try, went walkabout. The Kiwi half-back jumped the HJ Stadium fence and ran down the tunnel at the Wigan supporters' end, before finally appearing from the corner of the stand many seconds later. The claim was that Wood had eaten a hot dog on the way through!

Stevo's Hero!

Hot-dogging hat-trick hero Nathan Wood was the star as the Wolves downed Wigan

Stevo's Zero!

How many do you want? Widnes were full of them after being thrashed at Hull

Stevo's pearl

"It will allow us to put up more resistance to rugby union," French boss Jean-Paul Ferré on Perpignan's entry

Rd 12 results

Giants 6 ....Wildcats 38
Rhinos 34 ....Reds 6
Broncos 10 ....Tigers 12
Saints 35 ....Bulls 30
Wolves 34 ....Warriors 18
Hull 70 ....Vikings 4

If that was the case then Mrs Wood had better start feeding her husband a bit more supper. To munch your way through a hot dog in 30 seconds, with or without the mustard, is one mighty effort. Later, it became clear that he had tried to grab a hot dog from a more than bewildered vendor but, not surprisingly, was refused. No cash, no hot dog.

It is now becoming clear that Warrington players are keen to outdo each other in the try celebration stakes. I'm all for unusual antics - on the field, not off it. Thankfully, Nathan didn't get a smack from a disgruntled Wigan fan which would have left the game with one hell of a problem. Fair play to referee Steve Ganson, who told him to calm down.

Wigan would have liked nothing better because Wood was on fire. Three tries and two assists gained him the man of the match award by miles and no one was going to argue with Mr Hadfield and his media pals' selection this time. Nothing could have stopped him in this form. He ripped the Cherry and Whites to bits. After the match, Wood was asked if it was his best performance this year. "This year? Nah. Best ever," came the reply.

If that was the weekend's entrée, then Saturday's clash between St Helens and Bradford looked a tasty main course indeed. Having said that, not many gave the stumbling Bulls much of a chance and so it turned out with St Helens racing away to a convincing 26-12 half-time lead. And all that without a recognised hooker. Until he picked up a huge shiner, Jon Wilkin tried hard but once again Ian Millward's boys did well to grab two Super League points despite Keiron Cunningham's absence.

Early season Man of Steel contender Jason Hooper was outstanding. He bagged a hat-trick and split the Bulls' defence at will. His run from the scrum base in front of his own sticks for his second try was superb, although Bradford coach Brian Noble was seething about referee Russell Smith impeding scrum-half Paul Deacon. "It was a great tackle by Smith," he reflected.

TETLEY'S SUPER LEAGUE AT MON 31 MAY

	P	W	D	L	Diff	PTS
Rhinos	13	12	0	1	256	24
Saints	12	9	1	2	115	19
Hull FC	12	9	0	3	241	18
Bulls	13	8	1	4	142	17
Giants	12	8	0	4	6	16
Warriors	12	7	1	4	50	15
Wildcats	13	6	0	7	57	12
Wolves	13	5	1	7	-11	11
Vikings	13	4	0	9	-194	8
City Reds	14	3	0	11	-213	6
Broncos	14	3	0	11	-248	6
Tigers	13	1	0	12	-201	2

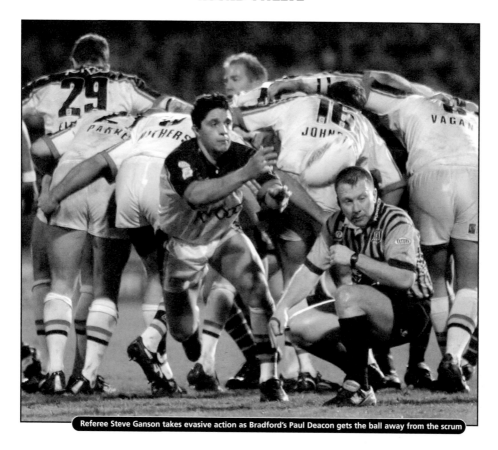

Referee Steve Ganson takes evasive action as Bradford's Paul Deacon gets the ball away from the scrum

This Bradford team aren't champions for nothing and Noble's half-time words of wisdom almost sparked one of the comebacks of the season. The return of Karl Pratt added some much-needed oomph to the side and his hat-trick in the space of 13 second-half minutes had St Helens hanging on by their finger tips. Could the Bulls snatch it or would Saints hold on? Paul Sculthorpe's late one-pointer steadied the ship and the home points were safe. It was a classic game in which Millward's side showed great character. In many ways it was a typical Super League match where every game is hard. I wish they would bring Halifax back. At least then we would have an easier week. Cruel, but fair.

Back in the relegation fight and there were celebrations for Castleford in the capital where the Tigers nicked it 12-10 in a solid arm wrestle with London. Both sides are desperate to avoid relegation and gave it everything.

Sadly on the Bank Holliday Monday, Widnes failed to deliver ANYTHING at Hull. It was the most woeful performance by a club in years and it brought about the Vikings' heaviest defeat of all time. Coach Neil Kelly said they should be arrested for pinching money. Not surprisingly, Kelly displayed the entire squad in front of the Monday media conference to "face the music".

Once again the rumours abound that Kelly is on the skids. Even he recognises that if his team produces another performance like that, he will be shown the door. Great game to be working in.

Stevo's
Babes!

Super League clubs make sure their dancing girls give fans plenty to cheer about!
Here are a few from Castleford, Salford, Warrington, Bradford, Wakefield & Leeds!

Wayne McDonald farms the ball out against Bradford

You're jestin', Iestyn!

SPECULATION, that was the buzzword this week.

It followed ever-increasing rumours that former Leeds star Iestyn Harris is about to quit Welsh rugby union and return to league.

The mere "fact" that Harris has purchased a new house in the Bradford area has had tongues wagging for quite some time. The Bulls, though, claim that they haven't approached him despite Iestyn's legal people being instructed to wind up his union contract. Leeds, his old club, claim that they have a water-tight agreement that Harris has to go back to the Rhinos. Either way, it seems that Harris IS desperate to get back into league.

On top of all that, news that former Hull CEO Shane Richardson has made a shock move from Australian NRL Premiers Penrith to bottom club South Sydney really set the nerves jangling on Humberside. Souths have also just sacked their coach, Paul Langmack, which suggests that Hull's Director of Rugby, Shaun McRae, could be flying back to Oz to join up once again with his old mate Richo. McRae was tight-lipped when I asked him if he was on his way. "Only rumours Stevo," he said. Could it just be coincidence that Shaun's new sponsored car was red and green - the Rabbitohs' famous colours?

All the gossip aside, one thing was for certain. Round 13 would bring us Super League's two biggest derby clashes: Wigan v St Helens and Bradford v Leeds. Mouthwatering stuff.

Stevo's Hero!

Wigan scrum-half Adrian Lam bounced back from his shock substitution last week to stun Saints

Stevo's Zero!

Salford centre Stuart Littler wasted a glorious chance to send winger Anthony Stewart in and seal a win v Huddersfield

Stevo's pearl

"I'll be picking the best man for the job" - new South Sydney boss Shane Richardson

Rd 13 results

Bulls 12 ....Rhinos 26
Tigers 18..............Hull 52
Wildcats 48...Broncos 18
Vikings 31......Wolves 10
Reds 18............Giants 25
Warriors 30......Saints 14

The JJB Stadium hasn't been a happy hunting ground for Saints and it proved so once again with Denis Betts and his charges shrugging off a poor display last week to bounce back with some of the toughest play this season.

The likes of Craig Smith and Terry O'Connor were outstanding. In a word, they "bashed" Ian Millward's mob. The forwards led the way with some ruthless running and tackling and Adrian Lam hit top form for the first time this year. The gamebreaker, though, was Danny Sculthorpe who once again produced some sublime off-loads, his first two producing tries.

It was tough throughout. There were 23 penalties - 17 for high shots - yet no player was placed on report and referee Ian Smith was even content not to call the two captains together when it looked like the local hospital was about to be put on overtime! This was Smith's first real test at the top level and I felt that he nearly lost it. Danny Sculthorpe nearly did likewise and, not surprisingly, his coach Betts substituted him before he could get himself sent off. He probably needn't have bothered. The merry whistle-blower looked for all the world like he had left his yellow and red cards at home.

Saints had no excuses. They were outplayed in every department and it became clear that the gamble of playing without a recognised hooker has finally caught up with them. Betts was proud of his boys and rightly so.

Driving back over the Pennines to Yorkshire, I reflected that if the high shots were going to continue I'd better stop off at the service station and buy a crash helmet for the big battle to come at Odsal.

As expected, another huge crowd was on hand and again they witnessed a Leeds victory that proved beyond doubt that the Rhinos mean business this term. Coach Tony Smith knew that a win would bring a rare double over the champions and remove any doubt that they can go all the way in Super League IX.

Andrew Dunemann was superb. He created all sorts of problems for the Bulls defence. His prompting, probing and kicking game came to the fore and provided an air of confidence not seen at Leeds for years. It was an all-round team effort, though. The Rhinos' defence was tough and uncompromising and with Matt Diskin and Rob Burrow eager to steal metres

Castleford's Waine Pryce had no joy when the Tigers played Hull

from dummy half it was no surprise to see the threequarter line enjoy space out wide where Willie Poching, an early substitution for Chris McKenna in the centres, ran riot. It was Poching's longest spell on the field for quite some time and he picked up the Tissot watch for best player.

Bradford showed glimpses of days gone by but they still lack bite up front. Winger Lesley Vainikolo tried hard and made more ground forward than anybody in the pack. That in itself tells a story. Could Iestyn Harris help? That was the burning question, as the Odsal faithful left the ground wondering where it has all gone wrong.

It also appears that the days of protecting your players have flown out of the window. Widnes coach Neil Kelly's idea that his players should face the press after their round 12 debacle clearly hit a raw nerve. In an embarrassing time for the club, the tactic obviously worked and the Vikings got some form back from nowhere to batter deadly local rivals Warrington. Like Widnes, the Wolves can't seem to produce good football on a regular basis.

Warrington coach Paul Cullen stopped short of naming the players he felt had played under par but the message was clear: "Buck up or ship out." Another boss to slap his players in public was Ellery Hanley who, like Kelly the week before, apologised to the fans for another inept showing.

Always a no-nonsense type of bloke, Ellery gave his Tigers charges a huge blast and claimed that he and coach Gary Mercer had prepared the side well. Yet never mind losing the plot, his team couldn't find the book for most of the 80 minutes.

Hull, meanwhile, just quietly breezed along, playing their usual solid stuff to let the big boys know that they will be around come play-off time. But can they keep McRae?

Stevo's Top 5
Hookers

1. MATT DISKIN
   Leeds
2. RICHARD SWAIN
   Hull
3. TERRY NEWTON
   Wigan
4. MICKEY HIGHAM
   St Helens
5. RYAN HUDSON
   Castleford

Stevo's Momento Rule!

4.2.4

A player running towards his/her opponent's goal-line may pass the ball to a colleague who is behind him/her but because of his/her own momentum the ball travels forward relative to the ground.

This is not a forward pass as the player has not passd the ball forward in relation to himself/herself. A good example is a high lobbed pass made by a running player.

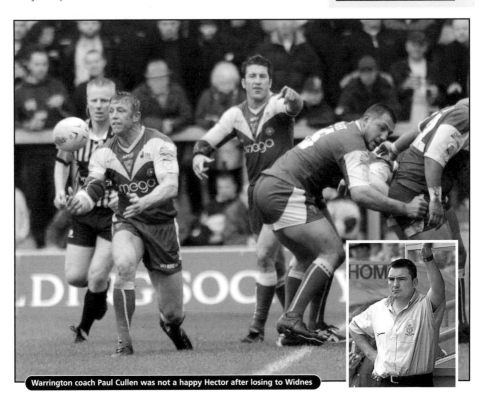

Warrington coach Paul Cullen was not a happy Hector after losing to Widnes

Ali Lauitiiti makes his Leeds debut against Widnes

Super McGuire's just on fire!

HOT, hot, hot. No other word for it.

And that was the weather, Leeds Rhinos and especially Danny McGuire. The Rhinos stand-off just blew Widnes away with some scintilating individual play and superb backing up. His five tries equalled the Super League record for tries in a match and steered Leeds into a commanding position at the top of the table.

Not that Widnes were completely outplayed. They gave a good account of themselves and really put their bodies on the line up until the last few minutes of the first half. But from then on in it was all Rhino power and the struggling Vikings were blown away.

Thankfully, the fans still managed to savour McGuire's effort despite one man trying desperately to grab the limelight away from the five-try star, namely referee Ian Smith. Smith, for some unknown reason, decided to make this game the one in which he would clamp down on and penalise every play-the-ball.

For years now, referees boss Stuart Cummings has gone along with all the coaches in that if a player makes an attempt to strike the ball back with the foot then it's okay. Play on. Yet Smith just decided to blow the whistle non-stop, ruining what should have been a good game. This stop-start approach by the merry whistle-blower spoiled the fans' enjoyment and frustrated the players. So much so that Leeds prop Barrie McDermott, who had been penalised for this offence, played the ball so slowly and definitely afterwards that it brought ironic cheers from the

Stevo's Hero!

Danny McGuire equalled a Super League record by scoring five tries in one match v Widnes

Stevo's Zero!

Ian Smith. The pedantic merry whistle-blower ruined the same game with his fussiness

Stevo's pearl

"Bradford have been categoric in denying any approach whatsoever" - Leeds' Gary Hetherington on the Iestyn Harris saga

Rd 14 results

Hull 28 ....Wildcats 24
Rhinos 48 ....Vikings 24
Reds 28 ....Bulls 35
Saints 52 ....Tigers 8
Wolves 42 .....Broncos 12
Warriors 40 .....Giants 18

crowd. Surely that should have awoken the official to the idea that he was spoiling the entertainment.

Fans pay big money to watch the players play, not the man in the middle strut around like a show pony. Even Leeds coach Tony Smith was upset that this tactic had denied his side the chance to get into any sort of rhythm.

Vikings coach Neil Kelly probably thought that a shock might be on the cards early doors. His side played well and stopped Leeds from gaining any momentum through some great defence. They looked odds-on to go into the break in front. Then again, he didn't anticipate the "Super Mac" display which blitzed them in the second half.

As I said earlier, I got plenty of stick from pundits and coaches last season when I pushed for Danny McGuire's inclusion into the third Ashes Test side against the Aussies. It was a dead rubber, the Ashes had gone so why didn't we give youth a chance? Those same people suggested it was making the Great Britain jersey cheap to "just hand out the red white and blue shirt".

What a load of rubbish. If anything, the fact that they didn't try some new blood indicated to me the old school approach, where it's nice to let players retire gracefully from the international scene. Come on, let's get serious here. Rugby league these days is a business, full-on professional. Sympathy shouldn't come into it.

I await with interest to see if McGuire's performance is still classified as "cheap" and whether he is still considered not good enough to play for his country. During the Sky commentary, I indicated that I thought the Leeds stand-off was on his way to becoming as good a player as the great Lewis Jones, a true Headingley legend. That was a big rap but I think he will.

Across the Pennines, the sweltering heat did little to enthuse me with regards to Warrington's battle with London Broncos. Poor old London have struggled. They have had far too many injuries, too many loan players and sadly a few that just don't shape up to Super League standard. Throw all that into the pot and you finish up with a pretty average stew. Even if it curbs the hunger pains it will never attract a Michelin star.

Warrington were also smarting in a different

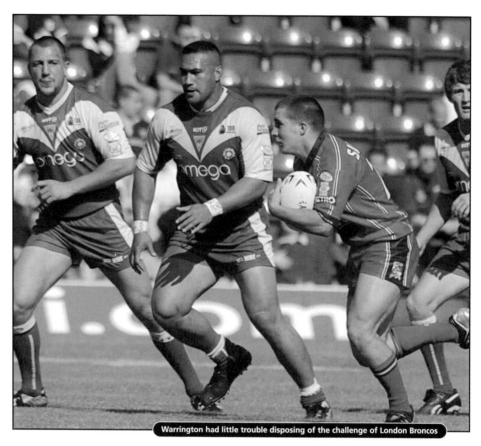

Warrington had little trouble disposing of the challenge of London Broncos

way. After a strong win over Wigan a fortnight ago, they fell foul to a rejuvenated Widnes outfit. Coach Paul Cullen knew that his team had to snatch the two league points if they were to have any chance of making the play-offs.

It soon became clear that there was only going to be one winner and a 20-0 half-time lead to the home side should have given Cullen plenty to smile about. It didn't, though. "We bombed far too many chances," he complained. "At one point, I felt we were going all out to create a new record of failed opportunities."

Paul was spot on. At least six or seven chances went to ground and gave London the chance to fight back in the second stanza. Once again it was Dennis Moran who scored to give them hope but they too started making mistakes and blew any hope of a late comeback.

To be honest, it wasn't a classic weekend for the televised games although the fans did get excited at other venues. Salford's mighty effort fell just short of shocking the Bradford Bulls and Hull struggled to hang on against Wakefield Trinity Wildcats.

Ellery Hanley's return to Knowsley Road sparked plenty of interest in St Helens but there was to be more disappointment for Castleford Tigers. People keep telling me that it's only a matter of time before the Tigers start to get a roll on and claw their way out of relegation trouble.

I'm still waiting.

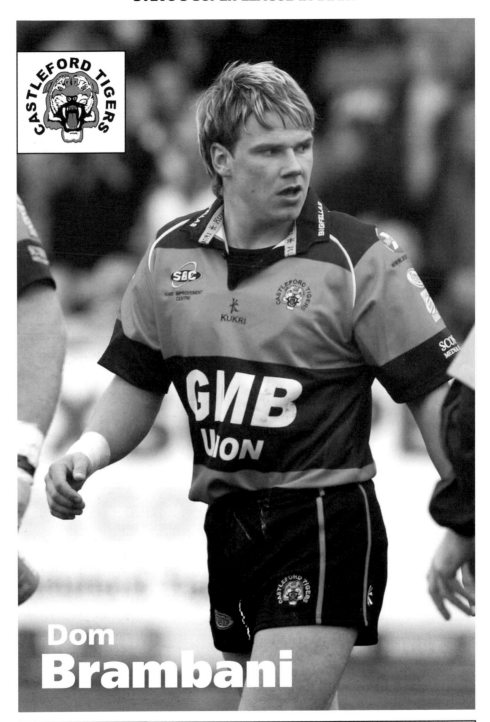

Dom
Brambani

AUTOGRAPH

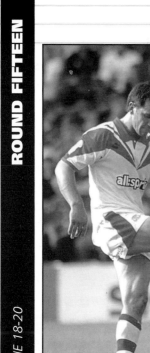

Paul Sculthorpe & Saints said adieu to Long & Gleeson

A game of heroes and villains

BOY, what a week.

The betting saga at St Helens finally got resolved with Sean Long and Martin Gleeson receiving three and four month bans respectively and a fine of £7,500 each.

That rendered Gleeson's Super League season finished, although he could still be in contention for Brian Noble's Gillette Tri-Nations Great Britain squad. Long, meanwhile, could be back for the Super League play-offs providing Saints get that far. It will be a difficult decision for new GB coach Noble who will have to think hard about including the Saints pair in his line-up.

Through the fact that both have had to pay the case's legal fees and that St Helens will not pay their salary for the time they are out of the game, you can see that the whole thing has cost them dearly. The Rugby Football League had to hit the pair hard and show some strength. That is exactly what they did, making it clear that all monies coming into RFL coffers would be used to help either a charity or junior development within the game.

It all left Saints coach Ian Millward without two of his biggest stars but, fair play to him, he just shrugged his shoulders and said, "life goes on." It did, too, as Saints blasted Widnes apart as if nothing had interfered with the week's build up.

The Vikings couldn't live with the team spirit and effort shown by a side who make it quite clear that they love nothing better than being the team everyone

Stevo's Hero!

Wigan skipper Andy Farrell led his side to victory despite a smashed up nose

Stevo's Zero!

A couple of Liam Botham mistakes cost London dear as the Broncos lost to Hull on the road in Leicester

Stevo's pearl

"I have been a right plonker," - Sean Long, after he and Martin Gleeson received bans

Rd 15 results

Bulls 40 ....Giants 12
Tigers 10 ....Wolves 32
Broncos 26...........Hull 42
Wildcats 21 ....Reds 20
Vikings 12 ....Saints 40
Warriors 26.....Rhinos 22

hates. Ian Millward uses it as a psychological ploy and his team responds wonderfully. Widnes, however, continue to make error after error which lets the opposition put them on the back foot time and time again.

Paul Sculthorpe put in a real captain's knock by taking responsibility for nearly every attacking play, whether it be at first receiver or searching for gaps out wide. He produced an all-round game and ensured the rest of the side followed suit. How he didn't win the man of the match award was a surprise to many. Our old friend Dave Hadfield, however, once again stunned the ranks with his selection of Nick Fozzard. Strewth!

Full credit to the man we call the Wildebeest, though. He knows that the game is not always about the star players who grab the limelight. Hard work is something Hadfield knows all about. Yet I couldn't help but smile when Fozzard was caught by the camera when the winner's name went up on the big screen. It appeared that he was flabbergasted.

Stevo's Top 5

Loose forwards

1. PAUL SCULTHORPE
   St Helens
2. KEVIN SINFIELD
   Leeds
3. SEAN O'LOUGHLIN
   Wigan
4. MIKE FORSHAW
   Warrington
5. LOGAN SWANN
   Bradford

"Who? Me?" he said from the sidelines. Well, I think that's what he said. It was no shock to Millward, though, who praised all his forwards for a job well done. "It has been a difficult week," he said. An understatement if ever there was one.

Yours truly enjoyed a good soak and a sauna in the hotel spa before taking off to Wigan for what turned out to be a classic. The disappointment of not shedding any pounds from all that effort was soon forgotten when the Cherry and Whites tore into Leeds as though they hated them.

What am I saying? Of course they hate them! Leeds soon realised this was going to be a test, especially after being drubbed at St Helens a few weeks ago. Some in the crowd, me included, thought that this would be the day the Rhinos showed Grand Final style nerves and overcame a hostile atmosphere.

Actually, the crowd was a disappointing one considering the table-topping team was on display.

Wigan hooker Terry Newton was in astounding form against former club Leeds. Above: Mike Gregory

Never mind, those who failed to show up missed a cracker.

Those who hate blood and guts should turn their head away now. It was one of those games where bodies were put on the line in a no-holds-barred contest. Boy, didn't they give each other some!

Wigan hooker Terry Newton was outstanding - run, tackle, guide, shout, he did the lot. Newton was so hyped up for this game that not even a fly, wasp or moth would have dared go near him. He was on a mission. Despite picking up a sternum injury, he threw his body into the fray with no reagrd for his own safety or that of anyone else. I don't know if Rhinos scream when they are hurt but I'm sure I heard something similar during the course of the 80 minutes.

Wigan's defence was superb. Leeds had seven continuous sets of six late in the game yet couldn't put their hosts away. Not surprisingly, Sky's rugby league producer Neville Smith continued to show Mike Gregory and Denis Betts up on the screen which lifted the fans to fever pitch.

I'd spoken to Mike Gregory before the match and he was in good spirits and said the treatment for his illness was working well and that he was on the road to recovery. This win was just the tonic he needed and full credit to stand-in coach

Stevo's Dream Team
Super League IX

1. RICHARD MATHERS
   Leeds Rhinos

2. LESLEY VAINIKOLO
   Bradford Bulls

3. KEITH SENIOR
   Leeds Rhinos

4. SID DOMIC
   Wakefield Trinity Wildcats

5. MARCUS BAI
   Leeds Rhinos

6. DANNY McGUIRE
   Leeds Rhinos

7. DENNIS MORAN
   London Broncos

8. ANDY FARRELL
   Wigan Warriors

9. MATT DISKIN
   Leeds Rhinos

10. STUART FIELDEN
    Bradford Bulls

11. DAVID SOLOMONA
    Wakefield Trinity Wildcats

12. ALI LAUITIITI
    Leeds Rhinos

13. PAUL SCULTHORPE
    St Helens

Betts who prepared the Wigan side to perfection.

It was a physical game and one that left Wigan skipper Andy Farrell with a bloodied broken nose. It was an injury that would have seen most players throw in the towel, but not Andy. He was bandaged up like something out of the Phantom of the Opera. At times he looked like the Lone Ranger, his effort was outstanding and left many saying how brave he was. A man in a real man's game.

On the other hand, those who witnessed the bandage being removed after the game might have suggested that Mr Farrell was stark raving mad. The sight of so much blood was enough to put you off your evening meal. It did little to prevent me from enjoying the odd glass of red, though, even if the old vin rouge did taste a bit more earthy than usual.

I raised a glass to both teams for a wonderful show and settled into bed to watch the replay on Sky. Vintage stuff all round. Cheers, lads!

The influential David Solomona drives Wakefield to a one-point win over Salford

Ryan Bailey helps Leeds to a hard-earned win over Hull

King of kings - Ali-lujah!

HE floats like a butterfly and stings like bee!

It's Ali once again, but not the famous pugilist - the Rhinos super signing Ali Lauitiiti. Boy, can this guy play! It was thanks to him that Leeds grinded out the win against Hull that kept them top of the table. Amazingly, Leeds snapped up the big forward to create tries yet, since his arrival, he has crossed the line five times. His ability to off-load in the tackle is one reason coach Tony Smith must be confident of reaching the Grand Final this year.

Lauitiiti has hands like shovels or, as Brian Noble puts it, holds the ball as though it's a peanut. The Rhinos were thankful for his contribution in overcoming a determined Hull side that, despite the growing rumours that they were about to lose their head coach Shaun McRae, played with much gusto and flair.

Friday nights at Headingley are wonderful occasions these days. The vocal fans in the South Stand are a dream for the team and hell for the officials. No one can convince me that the touch judge on that side of the pitch is not swayed by the pressure applied by those fans over each pass the opposition produce. Each 50-50 pass is accused of being so far forward we might as well be playing gridiron!

The plain truth is that these loyal supporters deserve some silverware. Apart from a Wembley success against London in 1999 the trophy cupboard has been bare. That won't change unless certain players can keep their heads when the pressure is on.

Stevo's Hero!

Ali Lauitiiti - the Michael Jordan of rugby league - was magnificent v Hull

Stevo's Zero!

Castleford centre Paul Mellor was already celebrating a try when Anthony Stewart came from nowhere to deny him

Stevo's pearl

"We need a winning culture" - Wakefield coach Shane McNally

Rd 16 results

Bulls 38 ....Vikings 30
Giants 35.......Broncos 22
Rhinos 28 ....Hull 24
Reds 30 ....Tigers 14
Saints 28 ....Wolves 8
Warriors 28..Wildcats 22

Leeds were leading 10-0 just before half-time and launching yet another attack at the boys from the KC stadium. Instead of putting another tight kick into the corner, however, skipper Kevin Sinfield elected to go for the power play.

When the ball was shifted wide, Hull's Richard Whiting was there to intercept and set up a rare sight in Super League these days, a penalty try. Whiting combined with Colin Best who sent Richard Horne racing for the line. His little grubber into the corner was superb and when Richard Mathers took him down without the ball the video referee had no hesitation in awarding the four points. That lifted Hull enough to see them go in at half-time 14-12 up, despite Leeds having had the better of the exchanges in the first stanza.

Controversy reared its ugly head again when referee Steve Ganson called for a knock-on (or a forward pass, take your pick) when the ball clearly hit Shaun Briscoe's head before Shayne McMenemy touched down. Why Ganson failed to go to the video ref is anyone's guess. With Shaun McRae away on family matters in Australia, Hull's stand-in coach John Kear was the pure diplomat. "These decisions tend to even themselves out," he said.

Leeds boss Tony Smith described it as a scrappy showing by his charges. At least they are still top of the ladder although I did make the point that Leeds won't win a thing if they don't find the killer 'Punch' and stop playing like 'Judy'. That was a comment that produced a fine reposte from Smith who introduced himself as Judy on our next meeting.

Talking of punch, the next day proved lacking in that department for the Saints v Warrington clash at Knowsley Road.

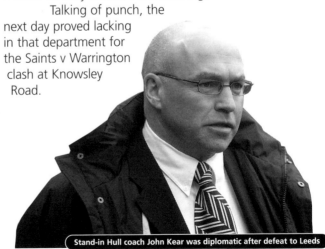

Stand-in Hull coach John Kear was diplomatic after defeat to Leeds

Willie Peters couldn't stop Widnes sliding to a defeat that saw the sacking of Neil Kelly

Forget it. Once again Widnes played poorly. They showed little idea other than that early prominence of new signing Peters. Wigan were too strong and showed how important it is to take chances. In the first 15 minutes, Widnes had several chances to score but failed totally. They then allowed the Cherry and Whites to snatch three tries from their first trio of real forays into the Widnes half.

Hooker Terry Newton was again outstanding, scoring four touchdowns. He could have had more, such was the Warriors' dominance. The youngster Stephen Wild was another to shine. He showed his ability to play in any position, on this occasion centre, and was no doubt letting the Wigan officials know that talk of them signing Mark Gasnier from St George-Illawarra had given him an extra incentive. There is talk that the club aren't eager to re-sign Wild. If they don't, there will be plenty of other clubs eager to snap him up.

Mark Smith was another to show his wares when coming off the bench. He was involved three times in the move that led to his try late in the game. A smiling Newton was on young Smith's inside as he raced towards the posts. With most fans expecting him to allow Terry a five-try total, Smith instead held on to the ball and scorched over himself. Rightly so. His effort deserved a crowning glory.

Little did he know that his try was to be the final nail in Neil Kelly's Widnes coaching coffin.

Favourite film:
Casablanca. Here's lookin' at you, Eddie.

Favourite TV show:
Have I Got News For You

Favourite other sport:
Golf

Favourite place:
Greek Islands

Favourite music:
Jazz

Favourite food:
Queensland Mud Crab with fresh Mango

Favourite drink:
Wine

Favourite car:
None. As long as they work, they're okay.

Favourite RL ground:
Headingley/KC Stadium

Favourite film star:
Peter Lorre

Favourite colour:
Red

Favourite animal:
Elephant

Favourite book:
Any Tom Sharpe novel

The **Stevo** file

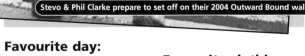

Stevo & Phil Clarke prepare to set off on their 2004 Outward Bound walk

Favourite day:
Sunday (usually day off)

Favourite clothing:
T-shirt/shorts (heaven)

Favourite hair-style:
Eddie's. You know, that cool Will Young look.

Favourite past players:
Tommy Harris was always my favourite, then Mick Sullivan and Billy Boston.

Favourite present player: Lesley Vainikolo

Stevo brings the 1972-73 Championship Trophy back to Dewsbury

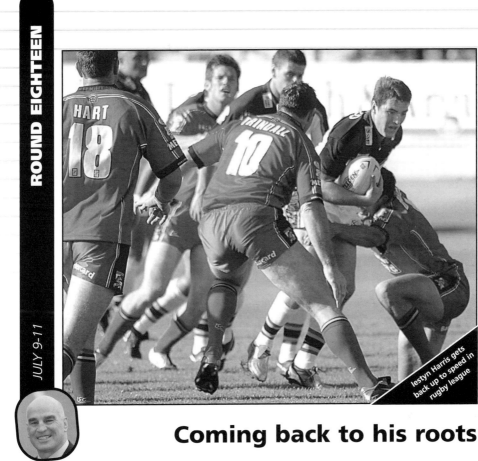

Iestyn Harris gets back up to speed in rugby league

Coming back to his roots

BUSMAN'S holiday for yours truly who found himself without a TV game on Friday night.

So it was off to Leeds where Gary Hetherington had kindly invited me to the Castleford clash. Great hospitality, even greater wine. Sadly, the game failed to live up to the same standards.

Danny McGuire was the star of the show and created all sorts of problems for the Tigers defence, although I just got the feeling Castleford were showing signs of getting it together for nearly the full 80 minutes. If they can show the same spirit from here on in and work for the whole game, who knows, they may just avoid relegation. Leeds played within themselves to chalk up yet another Headingley success. It will take a good side to beat them at home.

All eyes, of course, were on Sunday's clash at Odsal where the return of Iestyn Harris created much discussion among the supporters. Strangely, though, the expected huge crowd failed to materialise. Not that Bradford fans had much to cheer about, seeing as how Harris only entered the fray late in the game. Not surprisingly, the Welsh Wizard looked lost and was obviously struggling to get back to the pace of the game.

While many fans were disappointed at not yet seeing those silky skills he displayed at Leeds three years ago, they got their money's worth thanks to a brawl that involved umpteen players. Wakefield's Semi Tadulala appeared to get things

Stevo's Hero!

Leeds battler Willie Poching got a standing ovation at Headingley for his part in beating Cas

Stevo's Zero!

Castleford star Motu Tony had to have Motu on his shirt because the club shop ran out of 'y's

Stevo's pearl

"I see no reason why I can't be playing for Great Britain at Salford" - Reds prop Andy Coley who turned down Wigan

Rd 18 results

Bulls 36 ....Wildcats 26
Giants 26 ....Vikings 20
Rhinos 46 ....Tigers 14
Reds 16 ....Warriors 32
Saints 30 ....Broncos 10
Wolves 18............Hull 38
Rearranged Rd 8 match
Giants 8............Saints 50

going and then all hell was let loose, with Bulls winger Karl Pratt sent off for a king hit on his opposite number.

Not surprisingly, later in the week, Pratt was suspended for three matches. Wakefield pair Olivier Elima and Tadulala got two games each and Bradford's Leon Pryce landed a one-week ban that was overturned on appeal! The Bulls claimed that Pryce had been punished enough by his sin-binning and couldn't be punished twice. Word has it that the disciplinary hearing was as warm as the fight itself. Never gets boring our game, does it?

Back to playing matters and Wakefield put up a brave showing. They showed yet again that teams need to be in top form to beat them. Gareth Ellis, David March & Co took Bradford to the wire and Bulls coach Brian Noble was a relieved man after the game. I still feel that the Bulls haven't hit top form yet and Noble insisted that there is more to come. One thing is for sure. Bradford will not give up their Super League title without one almighty scrap.

Apart from his part in the bust-up, Pryce still fails to produce the goods for the full 80 minutes. His sublime skills are a joy to watch but he doesn't appear to want to produce more than the odd flash. In the opening minutes he created a great opening try, nice step, fend and inside pass that sent both me and the crowd into raptures, only to send us into deep depression throughout the remaining minutes.

Bradford need Pryce to impose himself more on the game if they are still to dream of Old Trafford success.

The day before saw struggling London visit St Helens in what was expected to be a walkover. Saints, though, had played in midweek against Huddersfield, where again Paul Sculthorpe's skills had steered them home. Three games in eight days is a big ask and it almost gave London the green light for a shock win.

Seeing that the Broncos had not played for two weeks and had spent a four day stint in an Army camp in Aldershot, one expected big things from Tony Rea's

Stevo's Top 5
Scrum-halves

1. DENNIS MORAN
London
2. ROB BURROW
Leeds
3. SEAN LONG
St Helens
4. BEN JEFFRIES
Wakefield
5. PAUL DEACON
Bradford

Paul Cooke torments an outclassed St Helens at Hull's Kingston Communications Stadium

conditions for the Black and Whites' crunch game against St Helens. A minute's silence before kick-off, in respect for Shaun McRae's late father, gave the game an emotional atmosphere. As did seeing Steve Prescott and his little boy lead the Hull side out to say farewell to both sets of fans and finally bring down the curtain on a great playing career. There weren't many in the KC Stadium who didn't have a lump in their throat.

Trouble was, once the game started, Saints played like they had lumps of lead in their boots as they struggled to keep up with Hull's pace.

A patched-up Paul Sculthorpe was doubtful before the game and it wasn't long before he had to come off injured. Once he had left the playing area, it was curtains for St Helens although Hull were in full control well before his departure. Prop Paul King was outstanding and must surely have lifted his chances for another shot at international stardom. Finally, his yo-yo tag seems to have been shed. He has performed out of his skin this season, with consistency the key. King is a rough, tough defender who off-loads with regularity. He did that throughout this game, picked up the Tissot watch and hopefully also picked up the vibes that his hard work and dedication will bring the rewards.

The Hull fans were over the moon. A thrashing of St Helens is no mean feat and that's what this was. Saints had no excuses. They were taken apart by a better side on the day but don't write them off yet. If they can overcome their injury crisis they will still be prodding the big boys in the eye come play-off time.

I was so elated that I treated myself to take away fish and chips before setting back off along Clive Sullivan Way and the M62. If you have never eaten Hull F and C, you haven't lived.

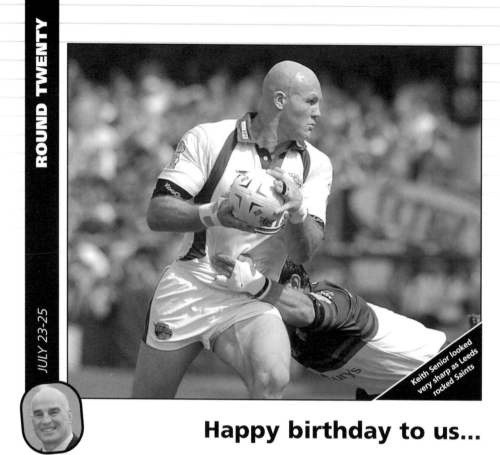

Keith Senior looked very sharp as Leeds rocked Saints

Happy birthday to us...

YOURS truly and Eddie Hemmings crashed through the 500 televised Super League games barrier at Headingley and, do you know, I didn't feel a day older. It has gone just like that!

When you throw in all the years prior to Super League's launch nine years ago, together we have rattled up over 1,000 TV games on Sky Sports. Not bad for something that many people said wouldn't last, eh?

To be fair, even Eddie and I find it amazing that we have worked together for so long. Not that we haven't fallen out from time to time; any relationship gets strained at times and ours is no different. I've sent him around the bend many times and he's poked that big nose of his into my face on more than a few occasions too. Yet we still stay good friends and we both agree that we would like to apologise for being beamed into your living rooms for all those years. If we upset you, tough!

Talking of which, the round 20 Friday night game was also tough for St Helens. It was hardly a game to celebrate reaching the 500 mark. Mind you, if you were a Leeds fan it was classic rugby league football of the highest order.

The Rhinos came up with some outstanding tries and gave the South Standers plenty to cheer about. When they look at the video of the game - and don't worry, they will - they will see that Saints just never got going, never tackled and never should have turned up. As soon as fullback Paul Wellens kicked dead in-

Stevo's Hero!

Danny McGuire's hat-trick v Saints equalled Paul Newlove's Super League record of 28 tries in a season

Stevo's Zero!

St Helens - literally!

Stevo's pearl

"We do not accept our place in the food chain" - Warrington coach Paul Cullen after signing Martin Gleeson from Saints

Rd 20 results

Bulls 44 ....Broncos 16
Giants 18........Wolves 34
Rhinos 70 ....Saints 0
City Reds 20 ....Hull 44
Vikings 25 ....Wildcats 24
Warriors 48 ......Tigers 18

goal from the start you knew something wasn't right for Ian Millward's boys. So it proved. They failed to score a point for the first time ever in Super League. Add to that the 70 points Leeds put on the scoreboard and you have to ask what's gone wrong with the 2004 Challenge Cup holders?

News that the club had sold its star Great Britain centre Martin Gleeson to Warrington only 24 hours before kick-off wouldn't have helped their mindset. With rumours that Sean Long would follow suit and be sold by the cash-strapped Saints abounding, we maybe should have guessed that things weren't right within the playing ranks.

Putting it simply, St Helens have lost their bite. No more do we see Keith Mason, Nick Fozzard and company taking control up front. There is no 'zing' in the threequarters. Even allowing for injury problems and suspensions, no Cup holders should fall apart to the tune of 70 unanswered points.

Leeds boss Tony Smith didn't get too excited about the result. Yes, he knew his team had played out of its skin, showing no repeat of putting the cue on the rack like they did the previous week against London. He is also intelligent enough to realise that Saints had a bad day at the office, just as he and his side did earlier in the year when Saints ripped the Rhinos apart at Knowsley Road.

Having said that, there was plenty to admire about the Leeds showing. Danny McGuire yet again exploded in typical fashion. So did Marcus Bai. A week's rest also paid dividends for Keith Senior, who looked the sharpest he's been all season. It was one-way traffic directed by my man of the match, Matt Diskin. The young hooker has come on in leaps and bounds this term. No more silly antics, he just gets on with his job which, on Friday's showing, is enough to at least be considered for GB honours.

McGuire picked up the Tissot watch from Dave Hadfield and the rest of the media. Who could blame them? His try-scoring burst left Saints floundering in his wake. Yet it was Diskin who was the architect throughout.

Is it a coincidence that the only two games Diskin has missed this year for Leeds were last week's draw in London and that awful bashing at Knowsley Road? I don't think so.

The guy has worked hard to express himself

Eorl Crabtree and Huddersfield had a hair-raising time against Warrington

both in attack and defence and is quickly becoming a genuine contender for Man of Steel. That may raise a few eyebrows but he has been consistent where plenty of others have been up and down like a fiddler's elbow.

One other pleasing aspect of the Rhinos' season has been the way in which Danny McGuire has proved he has the ability to tackle. Boy, didn't he come up with some bell ringers tonight! Many good judges felt defence was McGuire's only problem, suggesting he could score tries yet let in a few as well. Not any more.

It was hard to come to terms with the Leeds fans in the supporters club after the game. Not surprisingly, they were walking around stunned at the outcome and one even bought me a drink. Things really are on the improve at Headingley.

It was also nice of Leeds maestro Gary Hetherington, on behalf of the Rhinos bosses, to invite me for more refreshments later that night. You could say that I celebrated our 500 games milestone in big style.

Such indulgence deserved a late lie-in on Saturday morning and, for once this "summer", I enjoyed a stiff breeze blowing in the face whilst driving to the McAlpine stadium.

Yet again, I stared in disbelief at the lack of Huddersfield fans who turn up for a home game. Giants coach Jon Sharp has done a great job with his side and deserves more support. The club works hard at community and schools level in their area and they deserve better in a stadium that is first class. With the great signing of Brisbane and Australia star Michael De Vere for next season, Huddersfield are on the right lines. So, if you live in or near Huddersfield, tell the missus to go shopping

Jon Sharp has done a remarkable job with the Giants

early and take the family out for a great piece of entertainment. That's what we got when the Giants battled it out with a Warrington side bent on a win to keep their play-off hope alive.

A loss by the Wolves would have virtually sealed their fate and they worked hard to repell a tremendous opening 15 minutes by the Huddersfield outfit. On reflection, the Giants should have had the game in the bag during that early onslaught. Somehow, just one converted try was never going to be enough to see off a Wolves side that, after absorbing that initial period of pressure, clawed their way back and after the break took control.

Lee Briers was the key - when he fires the team does too. In contrast to Saints, the signing of Gleeson gave the club a huge lift and showed that they mean business next term. Coach Paul Cullen knows what his side can produce, providing they work hard for the full 80 minutes.

The win still left Warrington in the dog fight for a play-off spot yet, like London, they will have to play the top clubs in the final run-in. Again, tough is the word.

Thankfully, the rugby league bosses have come to their senses and realised that with two clubs being relegated next season a new structure has to be on the cards for Super League X. A system where evens and odds in this year's table will split into two different pools, where they will play each other over the last six matches, seems favourite. That would be a far more sensible approach all around. Things are looking up.

The battle for this year's relegation spot still rages on, although a Widnes win over Wakefield seems to have given the Vikings a little breathing space, especially with bottom two London and Castleford both losing this weekend.

It was a weekend of records in more ways than one. Yours truly made a hasty exit from the McAlpine stadium to enjoy a few more (the type you dance to) at the wedding bash of my Sky Sports colleague Phil Clarke over in Wigan.

No doubt that marriage will have brought a few sighs of despair from Sky's female audience but it truly was a remarkable weekend to remember. Here's to the next 500!

TETLEY'S SUPER LEAGUE AT MON 26 JULY

	P	W	D	L	Diff	PTS
Rhinos	20	17	1	2	398	35
Hull FC	20	15	1	4	357	31
Warriors	20	14	2	4	192	30
Bulls	20	14	1	5	255	29
Saints	20	14	1	5	152	29
Giants	20	10	0	10	-115	20
Wildcats	20	9	0	11	62	18
Wolves	20	8	1	11	-5	17
City Reds	20	5	0	15	-244	10
Vikings	20	5	0	15	-308	10
Broncos	20	3	1	16	-355	7
Tigers	20	2	0	18	-389	4

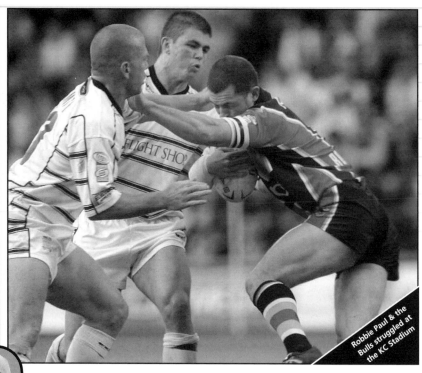

Robbie Paul & the Bulls struggled at the KC Stadium

One Hull of a bashing!

BEFORE this season began, not many fans would have suggested that Hull would do the double over champions Bradford.

That's exactly what happened at the KC stadium and even I was stunned by the power, skill and control displayed by Shaun McRae's men.

I had already asked whether Hull might struggle when it came to the play-off stages, due to the fact that not many of their players have experienced the cut and thrust of a top-six contest. Boy, didn't the side and their supporters put me in my place quick-smart?

If the amount of fans awaiting my arrival at the ground were anything to go by, my words of wisdom were not received all that well along the Humber! Plenty of words were expressed in, shall we say, an enthusiastic manner. Robust exchanges wouldn't really do it justice. They were sure that I would eat my words and what better way to make that happen than to rip the Bulls apart? That is just what they did, in great fashion.

To be honest, I feel that even the Hull fans knew their first try was somewhat forward. Despite the neat hands from Paul Cooke and Richard Whiting that sent Richie Barnett Jr in at the corner, how the officials missed the final pass to the winger was dumbfounding. You take what's on offer, though, and the home crowd went wild with glee. Bulls coach Brian Noble's face, on the other hand, looked distinctly unhappy at the decision. Full credit to Bradford, they knuckled

Stevo's Hero!

Veteran Castleford star Brad Davis returned to spark the Tigers into life at the Jungle

Stevo's Zero!

Frenchman Olivier Elima knocked on from the restart to stall a Wakey fightback at Leeds

Stevo's pearl

"I've learnt a hell of a lot" - Chris Thorman, confirms his return from Parramatta to Huddersfield next season

Rd 21 results

Tigers 42	....	Vikings 8
Hull 25	....	Bulls 14
Rhinos 46	.....	Wildcats 28
Broncos 22	...	Warriors 20
Saints 50	....	Giants 10
Wolves 46	...	City Reds 20

down and fought back, even holding an 8-6 half-time lead thanks to great play from Iestyn Harris who has settled back into our game quickly. It was the Welsh star who made the break to allow Shontayne Hape in for a well-taken try.

Bradford looked eager after the restart and had all the possession, field position and flair in a 15-minute period that should have blown Hull away. Yet time and time again they squandered opportunities. Lesley Vainikolo alone could have scored a hat-trick during this period but spilt the ball on every occasion. To miss so many chances in such a short space of time does little for your confidence and Hull slowly but surely grasped the chance to put the Bulls on the back foot. Cooke again showed his skills, a neat dummy and a hand-off on Jamie Peacock making room for him to send full-back Shaun Briscoe over for his 22nd try of the campaign. Briscoe has been outstanding this year, with Paul King and Kirk Yeaman not far behind him.

When Robbie Paul dropped the ball to allow Graeme Horne an intercept try that took the score to 18-8, you knew the Bulls were down and out. Noble was furious at the display, claiming it was the worst he has had to endure since taking over from Matthew Elliott.

"That hurt more than any other loss in my coaching career," he winced.

Brian may have been downhearted but I felt that the Bulls looked finally to be getting their act together with Stuart Fielden and Peacock finding form again. It was this pair, alongside Jimmy Lowes, who laid the foundation for last year's clean sweep of trophies. Don't write the Bulls off even if they will now struggle to clinch second spot, leaving them in sudden death football for the play-offs rather than the short route to Old Trafford like last season.

Hull just don't give in. They scramble back in numbers and run themselves into the ground each game. They must be confident of grabbing that second spot behind Leeds come the business end of the season.

Stevo's Top 5
Stand-offs

1. DANNY McGUIRE
   Leeds
2. JASON HOOPER
   St Helens
3. RICHARD HORNE
   Hull
4. STANLEY GENE
   Huddersfield
5. GARETH ELLIS
   Wakefield

Not surprisingly, after the game I was greeted with plenty of vocal fans wanting to stuff Stevo's boot in his mouth. At least I think that was the gist of the friendly abuse. After this showing, those black and white fans deserve some success and no team will look forward to playing them, especially at their new stadium. Hull fans know their rugby league, that's for sure. With my ears burning, I escaped onto the M62 for some peace and quiet.

That didn't last long either. The following day, those vociferous Hull fans were replaced with Tigers supporters eager to suggest that they would not be relegated as I drove into Castleford. They knew their clash with Widnes was important. So much so that plenty in the crowd were dressed up in Superman outfits to help their cause. The smattering of Widnes fans at the Jungle were hoping they'd brought some kryptonite to defuse Clark Kent's efforts.

The scene was set for a battle royale between two clubs fighting for their lives. While I failed to see either a

Phil Clarke & Stevo took plenty of stick from fans at the Jungle

plane or a bird, I did see a superman effort from Castleford who finally got their act together and blitzed a poor Widnes side who lacked ideas. Stand-in coach Stuart Spruce looked shell-shocked and his players weren't far behind him.

It just wasn't my weekend either, thanks to Eddie's insistence on bringing up the fact that both Phil Clarke and I had fired off a salvo a few weeks earlier saying it was not a smart move to bring back a 36-year-old veteran in the shape of Brad Davis. Boy, didn't that ruffle a few feathers?

Not least those of Mr Davis himself, who played out of his skin, showed skills and stamina of a 20-year-old and kicked Widnes to death. He won the man of the match award by a country mile. It was the Brad Davis show and he was loving every minute of it. So was Eddie, who probably brought up our criticism of the club five or six times during the commentary. On each occasion, as if by magic, Mr Davis produced another burst of excellent play.

Wow, did they give it to me big time. With a huge crowd standing under our TV gantry and baying for my blood in the background, Brad Davis received his man of the match award from Tissot and gave me and Clarkie a huge blast live on Sky Sports. Wonderful telly, though. So much so it left me with a huge lump in my throat.

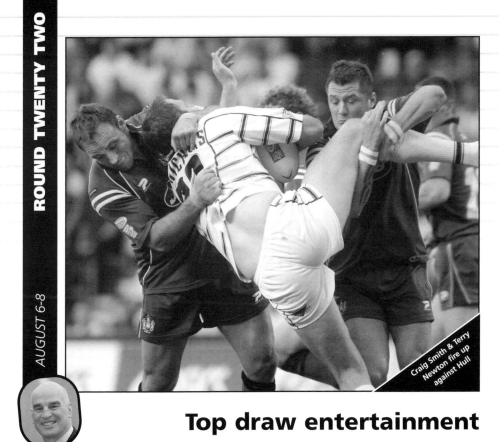

Craig Smith & Terry Newton fire up against Hull

Top draw entertainment

OH no, not Hull again!

Same motorway, but at least this time I was spared the trip east. Go west, young man, into the valley of pies and the JJB stadium, for a game that I reckoned would prove that the black and white boys could down another top club in Wigan.

All this talk of Hull having an "easier" final six games than their play-off rivals was starting to wear thin with their fans. You can't ecape the facts but it was yet more motivation to shut up the critics.

Wigan still hadn't been beaten at home all season and Hull boss Shaun McRae knew it was going to be tough. It was, so much so that Wigan should have blasted them away in the first 20 minutes when Hull just weren't at the races. With Andy Farrell once again leading the way from prop, that unbeaten record looked safe. Yet again, though, the guys from the east coast scrambled back in defence, tackled their hearts out and somehow defused Wigan's onslaught at a time when the Cherry and Whites were leading 12-0 thanks to tries from Danny Tickle and Stephen Wild. Hull had barely seen Wigan's half of the field, never mind been in it.

Mind you, the frustration was beginning to show in the Wigan players' faces. They should have scored at least two more tries in that commanding 30 minutes of the first stanza.

Funny game this! Ask stand-in Wigan coach Denis Betts who couldn't believe it when his team launched another high bomb towards Richie Barnett Jnr's

Stevo's Hero!

Jason Smith was in commanding form as Hull won a valuable draw at Wigan

Stevo's Zero!

With the tryline at his mercy, Stuart Jones knocked on against Leeds and Huddersfield's chances of staying in the top six were gone

Stevo's pearl

"He hit the ground running" - Wolves coach Paul Cullen on new signing Henry Fa'afili

Rd 22 results

Bulls 36 ....Wolves 22
Giants 10 ....Rhinos 42
City Reds 30.....Saints 20
Wildcats 39 ......Tigers 18
Vikings 24.....Broncos 38
Warriors 13 ....Hull 13

wing only to see the ball bounce into his arms, allowing the youngster to race away 60 metres towards the Warriors' line. Somehow, prop Craig Smith of all people got back to pull off a try-saving tackle. Not only did he tackle the winger, he then held him down and rolled him over a couple of times one way, then the other.

It should have been a penalty but referee Steve Ganson played the advantage and with Smith looking bewildered at not giving away the penalty, Hull quickly played the ball and swooped in for a try from Shaun Briscoe.

It was classic refereeing from Mr Ganson, who has copped a bit of flak from me over the years. This time he certainly got a pat on the back from yours truly. No doubt Shaun McRae felt the same way. Briscoe's try was a lifeline for Hull and they knew it. Despite being completely outplayed in every department, they were still in touch at the break.

Wigan restarted the match in the same fashion as the first half, by dominating proceedings and throwing the kitchen sink at McRae's men. Yet again their visitors dug deep to keep them out. Wave after wave of Wigan jerseys tore towards the Hull line but somehow it would not be crossed.

Then, when Richard Horne went over to level the scores, Hull had once again turned the tide and we were in for a thrilling finish. First, Farrell dropped a goal to take the lead, only for Horne to kick a one-pointer of his own with just two minutes left on the clock for a well-earned draw.

It had been a great game played in humid conditions. Despite Betts suggesting that it was a point lost for his side, one could safely say that Hull had their winning chances late in the game. Jason Smith provided some neat touches to steer Hull back into the match at a crucial time and his final run from dummy half could have won them the match had prop Ewan Dowes not dropped his captain's desperate pass as he dived over under the sticks.

Upon reflection, a draw was a just result with both sides providing excellent rugby and a real treat for the fans and TV viewers.

Given the hot, muggy conditions, shorts were the order of the weekend. The weather hardly helped the players and it even forced most of our crew into baring their knees to the world. Not a pretty sight. I didn't care, fashion has never been my strong point.

STEVO'S SUPER LEAGUE IX DIARY
ROUND TWENTY TWO

Sadly, my mate Eddie refused to join in the fun arriving at Huddersfield's newly-renamed Galpharm Stadium looking as much like a shop window dummy as he always does. Neat as a pin. The late afternoon kick-off should have helped but the humidity was unbearable to say the least. How those Giants and Rhinos lasted the pace was amazing.

Former Huddersfield coach Tony Smith returned to his old stomping ground confident that his new team would earn the two points and stay top of the table. So it proved with a dazzling first-half display that blew the Giants away.

Danny McGuire once again crossed to notch up 30 tries for the season but in such hot conditions and on such a fast track it was

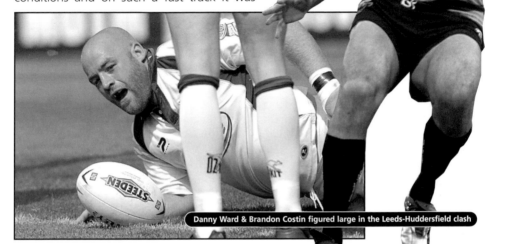

Danny Ward & Brandon Costin figured large in the Leeds-Huddersfield clash

surprising to see the effort from the forwards. Hooker Matt Diskin was again influential and Danny Ward just never stopped trying; an effort that earned him the man of the match award.

For Huddersfield, only Brandon Costin showed any real penetration and that was well after Leeds had wound up the match. Mind you, his solo try was a joy to watch. Giants coach Jon Sharp knew it was going to be difficult against the league leaders without the likes of Stanley Gene and Paul Reilly.

It would be too harsh to criticise the way Leeds tailed off midway through the second half. The heat was unbearable. So much so that Tony Smith suggested that the RFL should ensure all players get a chance to take on board more fluid. The loss drops Huddersfield out of the play-off zone and unless they get some of their injured players back soon they could fail to get back into the top six.

Nerves were the order of the day elsewhere where Salford shocked St Helens and London dinted the Widnes hopes of Super League survival. The Reds look safe now and the Broncos will also rest a little bit easier owing the fact that their win forced the Vikings down to second from bottom.

They shouldn't get too complacent, though. There's still six weeks to go! It's bite your nails time.

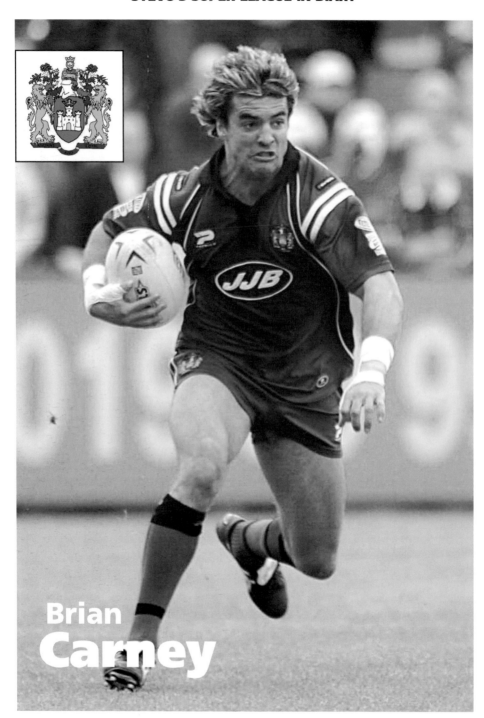

Brian Carney

AUTOGRAPH

Stuart Reardon goes flying but Bradford beat Wigan

Gore blimey! Bulls run riot

IT has been a week where a Harris tweed would have been helpful.

As it was, Wigan caught a cold from a different Harris, Bradford's new signing Iestyn, who decided to produce his best performance since his return from Welsh rugby union, leaving Wigan struggling to claim a top-two spot come the play-offs.

Despite looking off the pace in the first half, Harris scored twice to shatter the Warriors' dreams in the second. It wasn't Wigan's best showing, that's for sure. Yet it was something I have been expecting for a couple of weeks now, seeing as how they have had to continually turn out a patched-up team lately.

Captain Andy Farrell once again tried his heart out but neither he or his team-mates could stop the forward power of the Bulls pack. Bradford's forwards have always provided the springboard for the club's success. This season, it has taken some time for the likes of Stuart Fielden and Jamie Peacock to take control but, boy, they did in this game. Fielden's charging runs provided the Bulls with the position to cross for two early tries and from there on in Wigan were chasing the pack. They were ripped apart.

Full credit to the Warriors, though. They stuck to their task at a time when they looked likely to fall over. Mick Cassidy produced some excellent skills to send Martin Aspinwall in near the posts and when the impressive Sean O'Loughlin sent Brian Carney over we settled back for a thriller.

Stevo's Hero!

Dennis Moran scored three T-R-Y's against Saints in London's first-ever win at Knowsley Road

Stevo's Zero!

Widnes's failure to gather Salford's re-start cost them dear after Willie Peters had dragged them back into the match

Stevo's pearl

"I don't need much of a nudge to come to the UK" - Frank Endacott, on his way to rescue the Vikings

Rd 23 results

Bulls 38 ....Warriors 12
Giants 12..........Tigers 29
Hull 38 ....Wildcats 24
City Reds 14...Vikings 13
Saints 22 ....Broncos 28
Wolves 12.......Rhinos 44

The game was played at a cracking pace. Referee Russell Smith kept strict control of the ten metres, a big factor in the way the Odsal home crowd enjoyed proceedings. It would have been more painful for the travelling Wigan fans, though, who witnessed the Bulls going rampant in the second stanza.

It wasn't so much that Wigan disintegrated, it was a much better display from Brian Noble's charges that did the damage. The coach certainly deserves plenty of praise over his substitution policy. Not many coaches would replace the captain early in the game yet sending on Karl Pratt for Robbie Paul during the period when Wigan had started to get back into the match proved a masterstroke.

Pratt provided the sting that Bradford had been missing and lifted his side to another level. His kicking, passing and general open play was impressively controlled and while nobody could disagree with the choice of Fielden as man of the match, the former Leeds player was outstanding. For mine, he should be used more regularly by Noble from here on in.

Overall, one got the impression that the Bulls have finally turned the corner. The struggle to get it all back together has gone, replaced by the much more confident style of play we witnessed at the start of this season. Noble was happy with his side's performance, especially after the poor showings of the past few weeks. "Don't worry, we'll be in at the mix," he stated. He's right.

While Bradford were fighting for a top-two spot, London Broncos were battling it out at St Helens who, after the shock loss to Salford last week, were expected to blow the boys from London apart. It didn't work out that way, with Dennis Moran showing his class to steer Tony Rea's side to another unexpected win and maybe preserve their Super League status.

At the same time, it blew Saints' chances of improving their position in the league table. To say Ian Millward's men are in a slump is an understatement. That betting scandal and the sale of Martin Gleeson to Warrington seem to have blown their confidence apart. Either way, St Helens don't appear to be enjoying things these days.

It seems only yesterday that they were blowing Wigan away in the Challenge Cup Final in Cardiff.

It could be crunch time for Saints and that would also be a good description of what I received at

Halifax on Sunday. Along with some outstanding former internationals, I was invited along to play in the Matt King tag competition to help raise money for the badly-injured London Broncos junior.

Did I say "tag"? That is what it was supposed to be. Not surprisingly, it turned into a rough house. Graham Steadman, David Topliss, Lee Crooks, Garry Schofield, those were just four of the former league giants who turned out. Yet it was former Bradford star Brendon Hill who really caught my eye. And my ribs. And my leg. And my shoulder. And my head, as he decided to take the shortest route by running at, over and through me leaving poor old Stevo sprawling on the ground like a grounded whale. It was all worthwhile, with over £5,000 raised and the promise of more to come.

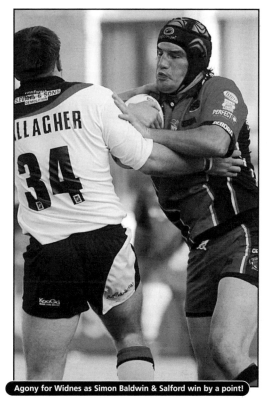

Agony for Widnes as Simon Baldwin & Salford win by a point!

Meanwhile back in Super League and it was off to Salford for the Reds-Widnes relegation duel. Talk about pressure. The match was an arm wrestle that went right down to the final seconds.

With Huddersfield going through a bad period, it was expected that Castleford would start their late run to avoid the drop by beating the Giants. That left Widnes more nervous than most and the early part of the match proved it.

Salford threw everything at them but somehow Widnes held out and then surprised the fans with a try from 20-year-old Jon Robinson against the run of play after great work by man of the match Jules O'Neill. The former Australian international looked likely to steer the Vikings to glory on his own. He was everywhere both in attack and defence. Widnes slowly but surely took a stranglehold on the match and deserved to be in control. Yet once again Salford broke their hearts when Joel Caine intercepted O'Neill's pass and sprinted 95 metres to put the Reds in front. O'Neill made up for his interception pass by storming over with less than ten minutes remaining to level the scores and his conversion from out wide put them in front. When Willie Peters slotted over a drop-goal to stretch that lead to three points, Widnes seemed likely to snatch a fully-deserved win.

Sadly for the Vikings fans, that wasn't the end of the story and when Andy Johnson scored with just minutes left on the clock, the City Reds had nicked the match 13-12. It was a victory that Salford didn't deserve and it left Widnes still in the dog fight with just five rounds to go.

Like the Vikings, I left the Willows nursing a few bruises. I would recover, though. Would Widnes?

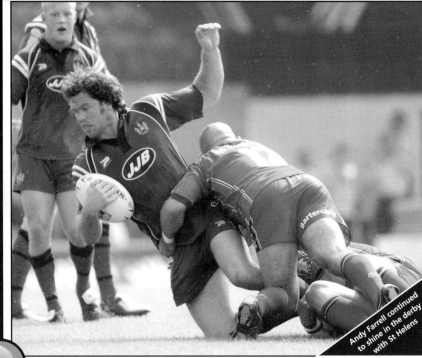

Andy Farrell continued to shine in the derby with St Helens

Love thy neighbour?

IT was a derby weekend to set the pulses racing.

Wigan v Saints. Leeds v Bradford. Who could ask for more?

Those games usually bring out the fire and brimstone from even the mildest-mannered players. At the JJB stadium on Friday night they lived up to their reputation. Boy, was this one a toughie! Spiteful, big hits, niggling, verbals, this match had it all. No prisoners were going to be taken, that's for sure.

Saints were looking down the barrel of a sixth defeat in nine games. They started the match with such gusto that it took your breath away, and a few players' heads into the bargain.

Referee Ian Smith was in for a torrid night in a game that looked all over after the first 20 minutes. It was during that time that Wigan crossed for three tries through Brett Dallas, Adrian Lam and Sean O'Loughlin. That must have surprised Saints boss Ian Millward who sent out the heavy brigade to crush Wigan early on, only to see his side give away silly head-high penalties in the opening exchanges.

The rough house tactics failed to put Wigan off their task, although when Terry Newton responded to a high tackle from Keith Mason with a neat upper cut one sensed this was going to be electric. Full credit to the Warriors. They held their nerve and their fists for those early stages and deserved their 18-0 lead.

St Helens had taken a huge gamble in giving teenager Scott Moore his debut in such a hotbed of a game. At 16, he became Super League's youngest

Stevo's Hero!

Castleford captain Ryan Hudson was outstanding as his side kept survival hopes alive by beating Hull

Stevo's Zero!

Terry Newton's off the ball challenge on Saints' Jon Wilkin earned the Wigan hooker a two-match suspension

Stevo's pearl

"We want to be a top six club not a bottom six club" - Salford Director of Rugby Steve Simms

Rd 24 results

Tigers 21..............Hull 14
Rhinos 40 ....Bulls 12
Broncos 34.....Wolves 26
Wildcats 46.City Reds 18
Vikings 24 ....Giants 18
Warriors 27 ......Saints 18

player, yet showed plenty of neat touches to indicate to me that he is one for the future. Indeed he is one for the present. It was his clean break that prodded Saints into action despite being one player down after the sin-binning of Jon Wilkin.

From good field position, winger Darren Albert showed his speed to send Jason Hooper in to open his side's account and give some hope of a revival.

As with most derbies, half-time can produce a turn around. Saints were far better after the restart. Young substitute James Roby replaced Albert on the wing and turned in a star display, while two tries in as many minutes saw Saints claw their way back to just 21-18 behind. They would have taken the lead if Mike Bennett's pass to Ade Gardner had not been around the winger's ankles. Who knows, if that one had stuck, Saints could and probably would have gone on to win. As it was, Wigan's late flurry saw Kris Radlinski cross for what proved to be the death knell for St Helens.

Not surprisingly in a tough encounter, tempers were frayed and Wigan could rue the fact that their fiery hooker Newton was put on report for a high shot on Wilkin with six minutes remaining. It was a bad one and nobody leaving the stadium was in any doubt that Newton wouldn't be around for a few weeks, a factor that could end Wigan's hopes of a top-two place in the Super League table.

Wigan stand-in coach Denis Betts felt Newton had hit the shoulder first. That is as maybe but the dazed look on Wilkin's face showed the swinging arm made its mark. Newton's action was nothing short of stupid at a time when Wigan had the game in the bag.

Once again, skipper Andy Farrell was outstanding. He must be making a huge run for the Man of Steel award. Not only did he work hard throughout, his distribution was first class. He may pack down at prop but he plays like a loose foward and was only upstaged by a magnificent performance from his stand-off and brother-in-law Sean O'Loughlin. Both coaches had lots to take out of it but you do wonder how it will affect Wigan if Newton gets suspended.

With my body still tingling from the JJB clash I dashed over the M62 with a spring in my step. Who wouldn't with Leeds v Bradford next on the menu? In honour of the occasion, I decided on a pricey Marlborough Sauvignon Blanc to wash down a five-star nosh!

Chris McKenna scorches over for Leeds v Bradford

Sadly the bill of fayre at Headingley didn't match that gastronomic good taste. As ever with the Yorkshire episode of derby time, there was a great feeling amongst the fans well before kick-off. Bulls and Rhinos shirts mingled with each other and the banter was good-natured. When Eddie and I had make up splashed all over the head to await the cameras there was a wonderful buzz in the air.

Thankfully the South Stand no longer has that old spiral staircase in front of the crowd where, for far too many years, yours truly has endured all sorts of antics including the odd coin and midget gem being launched at him. It is much safer now. We go via a back of the stand staircase but the wild South Standers still enjoy the banter of suggesting that I have eaten all the pies!

Bradford must have devoured a few themselves. They trundled around Headingley with little spark. My mate, John Stewart, a man who makes no secret of his enjoyment of food and has the body to prove it, suggested later that he could have done better himself. John is a Rhinos fan and knows his league inside out. Whilst enjoying the easy Leeds win, he was surprised by Bradford's poor showing.

"We were beaten by a better team on the night and we have to work at it a lot more," was Brian Noble's apt assessment, his wry smile suggesting that the Bulls were far from out of contention yet. The build up to the game was bitter and surrounded Iestyn Harris, whose return to Headingley was shrouded in legal threats to sue their former hero.

So much publicity of the wrong kind had seen Bradford put a media ban on speaking to Harris. Either way, the cloak and dagger stuff failed to work as Leeds ripped their neighbours apart. The Rhinos combined superbly to race to a 32-0 scoreline, giving the huge 21,225 crowd plenty to cheer or jeer about.

Danny McGuire crossed for two tries and

TETLEY'S SUPER LEAGUE AT MON 23 AUGUST

	P	W	D	L	Diff	PTS
Rhinos	24	21	1	2	508	43
Hull FC	24	17	2	5	375	36
Bulls	24	16	1	7	256	33
Warriors	24	15	3	6	173	33
Saints	24	15	1	8	167	31
Wildcats	24	11	0	13	79	22
Giants	24	10	0	14	-210	20
Wolves	24	9	1	14	-33	19
Broncos	24	7	1	16	-325	15
City Reds	24	7	0	17	-287	14
Vikings	24	6	0	18	-351	12
Tigers	24	5	0	19	-352	10

with Kevin Sinfield playing as his half-back partner and getting more involved, it was just a matter of how many Leeds would score. The end result was a thrashing for the Bulls but caution should be taken by the other Grand Final contenders.

Bradford only lost the second half 14-12 so maybe Mr Noble knows the Bulls are fighting back. Leeds, on the other hand, were superb and on this showing deserve to be favourites to win the Grand Final.

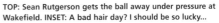

TOP: Sean Rutgerson gets the ball away under pressure at Wakefield. INSET: A bad hair day? I should be so lucky...

LEFT: Andy Coley & his Reds team-mates get to grips with Leeds

BELOW LEFT: Cliff Beverley had a big season at the Willows

BELOW RIGHT: Salford's Maori fan club in full voice

RIGHT: Michael Korkidas gets stuck into Widnes in typically robust style

INSET: Wakefield mascot Daddy Cool

BELOW: The Wildcats coaching dream team - Tony Smith & Shane McNally

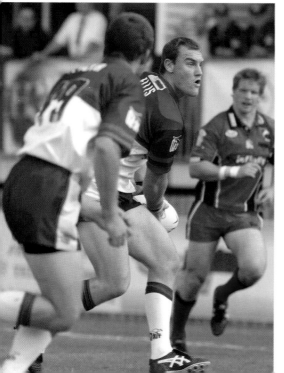

ABOVE: David March holds the ball steady ahead of a Wakefield conversion
BELOW: Sid Domic tears through the heart of Castleford's defence
RIGHT: Gareth Ellis leads the Wildcats attack at the Willows

LEFT: Ben Westwood tests the Wakefield defence as the Wolves kick-off life at the Halliwell Jones Stadium

BELOW LEFT: The Warrington cheerleaders line up for action

BELOW RIGHT: A panoramic view of the new stadium

BELOW: Martin Gleeson looks on after joining Warrington Wolves for Super League X

RIGHT: Danny Lima made a massive impact in the ranks of the Primrose & Blue

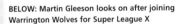

WIDNES

TOP LEFT: Matt Whittaker on the charge at Castleford

TOP RIGHT: Neil Kelly

RIGHT: Shane Millard finds a gap in the Wakefield defence at the ASS Stadium

BELOW LEFT: A delighted Frank Endacott keeps Widnes in Super League

BELOW RIGHT: Deon Bird goes over for a try at Wigan in high-flying style

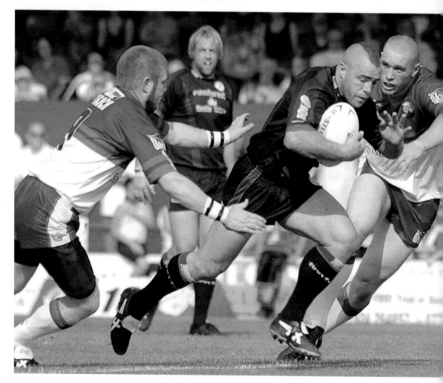

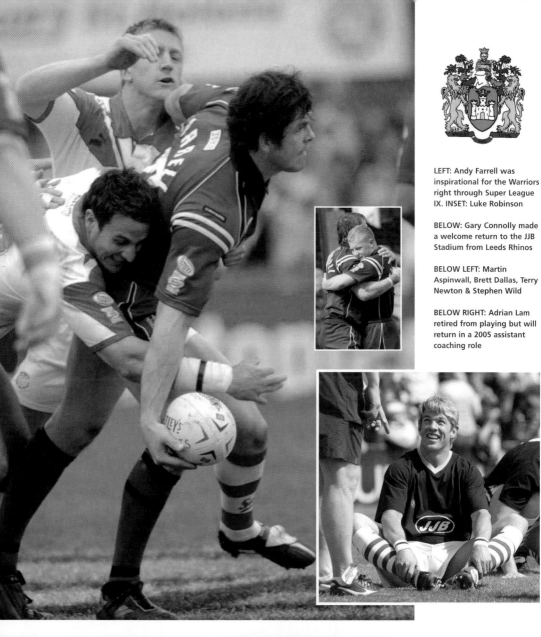

LEFT: Andy Farrell was inspirational for the Warriors right through Super League IX. INSET: Luke Robinson

BELOW: Gary Connolly made a welcome return to the JJB Stadium from Leeds Rhinos

BELOW LEFT: Martin Aspinwall, Brett Dallas, Terry Newton & Stephen Wild

BELOW RIGHT: Adrian Lam retired from playing but will return in a 2005 assistant coaching role

LEFT: Keith Senior, Jason Hooper, Robbie Paul, Richa[rd] Swain, Kris Radlinski & Gareth Ellis line up to represent Leeds, St Helens, Bradford, Hull, Wigan & Wakefield at the launch of the Super League play-offs

BELOW LEFT: St Helens we[nt] out in an opening round defeat to derby rivals Wig[an]

BELOW RIGHT: Rhinos pair[ing] David Furner & Keith Senio[r] conspire to halt Kevin Brow[n]

Super League IX Play-Offs

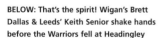

BELOW: That's the spirit! Wigan's Brett Dallas & Leeds' Keith Senior shake hands before the Warriors fell at Headingley

BELOW RIGHT: Wakefield Trinity Wildcats stunned Hull FC at the KC Stadium before being shot down at Wigan's JJB Stadium

uper League Grand Final 2004

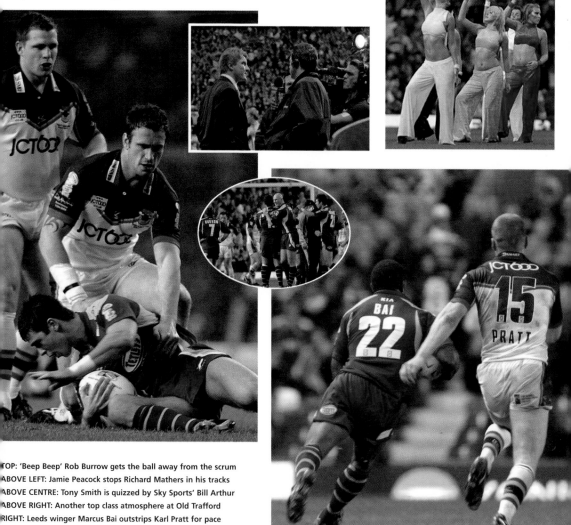

TOP: 'Beep Beep' Rob Burrow gets the ball away from the scrum

ABOVE LEFT: Jamie Peacock stops Richard Mathers in his tracks

ABOVE CENTRE: Tony Smith is quizzed by Sky Sports' Bill Arthur

ABOVE RIGHT: Another top class atmosphere at Old Trafford

RIGHT: Leeds winger Marcus Bai outstrips Karl Pratt for pace

Champions 2004

Kevin Sinfield has a field day against Castleford

Cas cats get Rhinos in a flap

KINGS of the Jungle or pussy cats?

That was the question as the Tigers went to Headingley to try and stave off relegation and spoil the party for a Leeds oufit ready to claim their first League Leaders Shield in 30-odd years. After Castleford's shock win over high-flying Hull last week, Rhinos coach Tony Smith was taking nothing for granted and expected a tough encounter. He got one too as the Tigers threw everything at Leeds in the hope they may crack just the way Hull had.

With so much publicity about the Leaders Shield one could expect Leeds to be a little nervous. They weren't. After absorbing the Tigers onslaught, the Rhinos clicked into top gear and blew their opponents away.

Tony Smith is a shrewd coach and made sure the League Leaders Shield was NOT going to be presented to the team if they won. "It's nice to say we have won silverware for our fans but we targeted the Grand Final and the Super League trophy at the start of the season. We still have to concentrate on that alone." Wise words seeing how his brother Brian had experienced being a table-topper in Australia, yet failed to nail the big one.

We at Sky Sports were lucky enough to hold the Shield and a nice piece of work it is. We wanted to film the trophy before kick-off but it was soon whipped away to RFL headquarters after the shoot. Sad that, as it would look quite nice on the sideboard of my London flat!

Stevo's Hero!

Leeds centre Chev Walker scored four tries as the Rhinos won the League Leaders Shield

Stevo's Zero!

Huddersfield prop Jim Gannon was named as having conceded the most penalties in Super League IX so far - 30!

Stevo's pearl

"The boys tell me they are ready to step it up a gear" - Rhinos coach Tony Smith

Rd 25 results

Rhinos 64.........Tigers 12
Broncos 16...Wildcats 24
City Reds 6.....Wolves 32
Saints 48..........Giants 12
Vikings 20....Warriors 16
Hull 12................Bulls 26

As for Castleford, they would probably have preferred to have been in the capital rather than trying to stem the onslaught which, for a second week in succession, was tremendous. And all without Danny McGuire and Chris McKenna. Yet again that allowed Kevin Sinfield to play the link role, a move that has helped the Leeds skipper get his confidence and attacking flair back on track.

Sinfield was awesome as he teased Castleford time and time again with superb options and off-loading. With big Ali Lauitiiti running inside the centres it was easy to see why the likes of Keith Senior ran riot in the early stages of the match.

Lauitiiti twice linked with his captain to put Senior through and the same approach provided Rob Burrow with copycat tries eight and ten minutes into the game. From there, it was one-way traffic. Like the week before against Bradford, the game was all wrapped up at half-time with a 34 - 6 scoreline.

Chev Walker crossed for four tries in a good display of finishing although that was not enough to snare the man of the match award. Yet again Dave Hadfield and the media spurned Walker's efforts and slapped the Tissot watch on Senior's wrist. That surprised most at the game, including Senior himself, doubly so when you considered the majestic way Sinfield had plotted the Tigers' downfall.

But this Leeds side is not about individuals. It is teamwork that has forged success and the players and coach know it. What a smile Gary Hetherington must be displaying these days, for it was Gary who snatched Smith from Huddersfield when it looked likely the Australian was going elsewhere.

Plenty of Rhinos fans were stunned at seeing last year's coach, Daryl Powell, shunted into a coaching directors role or whatever title he holds these days. These days, though, Smith is flavour of the month. As is Mr Hetherington, who even receives the odd slap on the back, a rarity for a CEO.

As after most games, I wandered into the

Stevo's Quiz
Answers
from page 26
1) Whitehaven; 2) Richard Swain; 3) Perpignan, or UTC as they are currently known; 4) London Broncos; 5) Danny McGuire; 6) Canterbury Bulldogs; 7) Sean Long; 8) Mark Gasnier; 9) James Graham; 10) Steve Prescott. 22 points for England v France in 1996 and 14 points for Ireland v Samoa in 2000.

Jules O'Neill showed plenty of flair when struggling Widnes shocked play-off hopefuls Wigan

Supporters Club for a relaxing drink after the game, to be greeeted with the chant of: "We are the champions!" League Leaders, yes, not title holders yet. Although one couldn't argue with the confidence of the fans, who for many years have seen a false dawn turn horribly black come crunch time.

Even Big John the ardent Leeds supporter was cagey. "It's the Big One we want and I won't be satisfied until we get it," was his cry. Yet he was happy enough to shout me a drink at the bar which only proves that the times they are a-changing out Headingley way.

Sadly, the Tigers fans trudged out of the ground hoping that Widnes would at least be taken to the cleaners by Wigan the following day. Hope springs eternal, they say. At the Halton Stadium, though, Wigan were lacking the suspended Terry Newton as expected and Craig Smith. Those were two battlers Wigan could ill afford to be without and Widnes knew it.

It's amazing how one loss of concentration can turn, not just a game, but a season. Newton's swinging arm could have cost the Warriors a home tie in the play-offs. In a sensational turnaround, Andy Farrell's men never got a look-in as Widnes bumped, pushed, smacked, hammered and smashed Wigan into submission.

With hooker Shane Millard leading the way and Jules O'Neill providing the flair, the VIkings took control early on and when Steve McCurrie crawled out of the tackle to lunge for the line you sensed an upset.

O'Neill was a thorn in his former club's side. His prompting confused Wigan no end and when he tagged on a penalty just before the break to take them into a 8-0 lead, a fairy story was about to unfold.

Where was this style of play before? Widnes were showing defensive qualities to match Super League's best. Not once did Wigan get a clean break in 60 minutes and with a 22 out of 24 completion rate you wondered if you were watching the same side of a few months before.

Caretaker coach Stuart Spruce is a quiet bloke who has at least brought some pride back into an outfit that looked intent on getting the season over and done with as soon as possible now they are looking for survival. While those Tiger fans were crossing their fingers in the hope that Wigan would fire in the second half you just knew it was going to be Widnes's day.

No doubt the introduction of former New Zealand and Wigan coach Frank Endacott was a factor. "Happy Frank" is the kind of bloke you like going to lunch with. While not everyone at Widnes took too kindly to the Kiwi being brought into the fray, the truth is it's working and Frank and Spruce could well form a dynamic duo in the future.

Denis Betts was disappointed with his players' efforts. "We started to do the right things too late," was the cry. Three late tries in the space of 14 minutes gave them some

Frank Endacott made an immediate impact at the Halton Stadium on his UK return

hope but it would have been a cruel blow if the Warriors had snatched victory. Wigan's injury problems have taken their toll and they look tired. Throw in that swinging arm from Newton the week before and you soon realise what a brain explosion can do to a side.

Widnes, on the other hand, now know that they hold their destiny in their own hands and don't have to rely on other results going their way. A home win against Castleford in two weeks time could hold the key. I wonder which way it will turn? One thing's for sure. Our game never gets boring, does it?

On to Bank Holiday Monday and while I don't know much about engines or cars, I do know that Bradford have had a stop-start season. I also know that Bulls coach Brian Noble is a fine driver and that he knew there would be plenty of bumps to negotiate as his side drove over to Hull.

In front of another big crowd, the home fans were far from convinced that another win over the Bulls was there for the taking. Hull also were struggling to hit top form and many fans were wondering if their side had hit the brick wall. So, it was a nervous set of supporters who awaited the battle and what a fine scrap they got.

The feud between Jason Smith and Stuart Fielden was always going to test merry whistle-blower Steve Ganson and, not surprisingly, Fielden was put on report

Stuart Fielden & Jason Smith came to blows when Hull met Bradford

for what looked like a high tackle on the Hull skipper. Leon Pryce was another to be subjected to the RFL disciplinary for lashing out with his boot. Both escaped any further punishment, with the RFL executive saying they had no case to answer later on in the week. That would have been scant reward for Smith who also got into a tangle with Fielden later in the game, when a punch-athon ensued sending the Hull captain into a stagger and leaving him battered with blood spouting out all over his face. There was no doubt who won that little tussle with Smith displaying a face like a crushed strawberry.

Noble was pleased with the win and the way his side fought back to overcome Hull's early lead. His opposite number Shaun McRae, though, felt his team were badly done by with two video referee decisions going against them at crucial moments in the game.

Bradford were certainly lucky to have what looked a clear try by Richie Barnett Jnr overturned just before the break. I felt sure that if that try had stood Bradford would have struggled to come back into the match. As it was, it gave them enough breathing space to settle down in the dressing room and play some vintage football in the second stanza.

Generally, it was a spiteful game that needed something special to produce a win. After trailing Hull 10-0, the Bulls found it in Lesley Vainikolo who crossed for a hat-trick to steer Bradford home.

It was a victory that piled even more pressure on Hull to hang on to second place in the table, while leading Bradford to think that they might just sneak that vital spot themselves.

Paul
Reilly

AUTOGRAPH

Wigan had more reason to celebrate against Leeds

Pies down for a full house

MY nerves were on edge and I only watch and comment on the games!

I just knew there would be tension all around when I arrived at Wigan for their vital clash with the Rhinos and I wasn't far wrong. Some Wigan fans were still despondent over last week's loss to Widnes and even felt they would be no match for a Leeds side that just six days before had won the League Leaders Shield. Tony Smith's men, though, were far from confident. For some unknown reason the Rhinos find it hard to travel over the Pennines. Lancashire is not a good hunting ground for them, especially when it comes to playing against the big boys. So it proved again with a gutsy display from the Cherry and Whites that saw them take the lead against the favourites.

And what a try it was! Brian Carney took the ball deep within his own half and then raced away while eluding three would-be tackles. The final attempt, from Leeds full-back Richard Mathers who went high instead of taking the winger's legs, should have stopped him. However, nobody should take anything take away from the Irishman's effort in scoring what could be the try of the season.

It didn't take long for the Leeds players to realise that Wigan had upped the tempo since last week's defeat. They also had the knowledge that it was Wigan who last beat Leeds in June ringing in their heads. It was a battle royale. With Craig Smith and Andy Farrell, in particular, both showing great strength and skill, it looked odds on that Wigan would run away with it.

Stevo's Hero!

Salford fullback Karl Fitzpatrick scored two tries as the City Reds all-but condemned Castleford to relegation

Stevo's Zero!

Sin-binned Hull star Richard Horne epitomised the way the Airlie Birds have lost their way lately

Stevo's pearl

"It's a good job I have always been clean-shaven" - Paul Sculthorpe, the new face of Gillette!

Rd 26 results

Bulls 60 ....Broncos 18
Tigers 22.....City Reds 24
Giants 27 ....Hull 20
Wildcats 40......Vikings 6
Wolves 24 ....Saints 26
Warriors 12.....Rhinos 12

At 8-0 up after just ten minutes it was little wonder that Leeds looked shocked. Gone was the confident manner of weeks before and they couldn't match the solid Wigan defence who, in old-fashioned terms, gave it to them big style. The home crowd was loving it.

For their part, Leeds were happy to hear the half-time hooter, especially coach Smith who at least knew that his side had repelled a late first-half onslaught with some desperate defence, to hold out "certain" scorers Adrian Lam, Danny Tickle and Martin Aspinwall.

It was a different Rhinos outfit that faced Wigan in the second stanza. Some sublime running from Matt Diskin created a try for Danny McGuire near the posts and Kevin Sinfield's conversion took it to 8-6. Now it was Wigan's turn to hold on as Leeds went close three times through Jamie Jones-Buchanan, Danny Ward and Keith Senior. Farrell kicked a penalty to pull Wigan away again but nothing was going to stop the next Rhinos effort.

First, Ali Lauitiiti and Chris McKenna combined to keep the ball alive before sending McGuire dancing through on the arc. His speed dragged the defence into the corner and gave him the room to send Mathers towards the line. The full-back, in turn, off-loaded to Senior who gave the final pass to McGuire who had supported well to bag his second of the night. Wonderful stuff that even had the Wigan fans applauding. Sinfield's conversion put Leeds in front for the first time before the last 30 minutes provided some classic rugby league football. Rough and tough with no prisoners taken.

After another Farrell penalty tied the scores at 10-10, both sides went looking for that crucial one-pointer - much to my delight! Plenty of coaches have taken me to task over my insistence that a drop-goal is a vital weapon at any time of the game, yet both sides were incapable of setting up in a decent position to win the match. Wigan had better field position yet turned down chances time and time again, opting for individual kicks for glory rather than using common sense.

In the end, a draw was a fair reflection of a game that Wigan had dominated in the first half, Leeds in the second. Sadly the game had some of the shine taken off it by what appeared to be a bite from Ryan

STEVO'S SUPER LEAGUE IX DIARY

Bailey on Mark Smith but the Wigan hooker declined the referee's offer of putting it on report. Two days later, the issue was resoved when the RFL decided there was insufficient evidence to take the matter any further. Leeds should feel pleased that they fought back and showed they will still be the side to stop for the Super League trophy.

No trophies on offer down the bottom end of the table, of course, no silverware at stake there. Only your livelihood and Castleford and Salford both knew it, played like it and came up with a thriller at the Jungle.

Desperate is the only word to describe a game that flowed first one way then the other, with more nerves on display than classy play. For the third time this season, the Tigers threw away a 12-0 lead to succumb to a club for whom an eventual 24-22 victory secured their place in Super League X. While Salford coach Karl Harrison and his team ran to their loyal supporters after the final whistle, the Tiger fans trudged out, heads bowed and with tears in their eyes.

With only seconds remaining of the first half, Castleford had Salford on

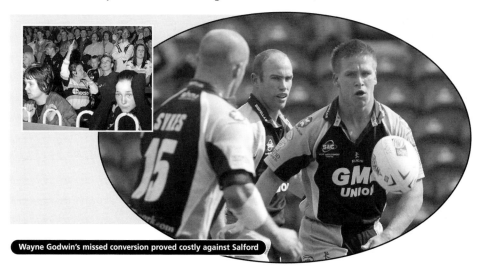

Wayne Godwin's missed conversion proved costly against Salford

toast and when Reds centre Stuart Littler was sin-binned one expected the Tigers to run riot. Sadly for the Cas fans, though, it was Salford who took their chances with the outstanding Karl Fitzpatrick setting up field position for hooker Malcolm Alker to score under the sticks just before the half-time hooter. That gave Salford a huge boost and they looked the more positive side as both teams left the field.

It was a real old ding-dong after the break with both sides scoring tries to stay in the game. When Fitzpatrick crossed late for his second Castleford looked doomed, although they did have a chance to level the scores when Paul Mellor sealed his hat-trick on 70 minutes, but Wayne Godwin missed his conversion attempt from out wide and Salford held on.

Eddie and I were off our seats for the entire game such was the pressure and intensity. Not surprisingly, plenty of the Tigers fans aimed their frustration at me. Being polite, I turned a deaf ear but the air was blue. Why? I haven't missed a tackle, knocked on etc for over 25 years. Losing is tough to take, though, and I was quick to tell one crying young boy that his favourite team weren't relegated yet.

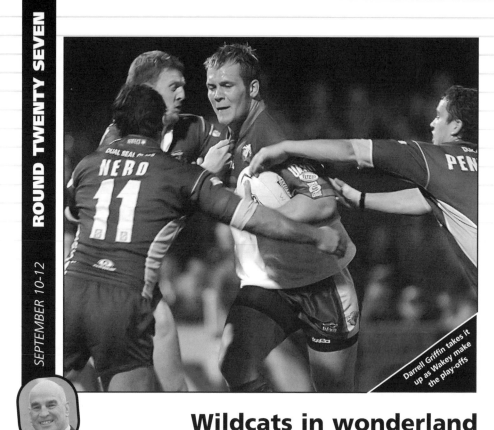

Darrell Griffin takes it up as Wakey make the play-offs

Wildcats in wonderland

DON'T you just love a celebration?

A time to enjoy success, a party, a cake and smiling faces all around. So it was with great delight that I drove to Wakefield in the knowledge that the Wildcats would be celebrating making the play-offs for the first time. I'm not good at maths but even I knew that Huddersfield couldn't win their last matches by the 100-odd points needed to deny Wakefield.

Even the Hertz car company seemed to feel this weekend was something special seeing as how they gave me the keys to a souped-up sports car by the name of a "Crossfire". It looked sleak, fast and attractive, all the things yours truly ain't! It took me ten mintues to get into the damn thing and even longer to get out.

Wakefield wanted to secure sixth spot with a flourish even though they knew the much-improved Giants would be tough, especially with the likes of Brandon Costin and Stanley Gene back on top form as Hull will testify. It did look sad for the Giants in the opening exchanges, though, when Wakefield just took control. With better field position, a glut of possession and an air of confidence we have seen so often this year from the Wildcats, one got the early impression this was going to be easy. Far from it. Huddersfield stood firm, scrambled back time and time again and then turned the game into an arm wrestle with tough uncompromising tackles and the odd fracas.

One thing you can be sure of when either of the March twins play is that

Stevo's Hero!

Francis Maloney's 30m drop-goal proved just enough to beat Widnes and take the relegation scrap to the last weekend

Stevo's Zero!

Huddersfield full-back Paul Reilly's sin-binning summed up the Giants' display as Wakefield made the play-offs

Stevo's pearl

"Leeds and Bradford will have to work really hard to play Saints in the Grand Final" - Ian Millward

Rd 27 results

Broncos 22...Warriors 26
City Reds 8 ....Hull 12
Saints 19 ....Rhinos 25
Wildcats 21 .....Giants 20
Wolves 27 ....Bulls 28
Vikings 6 ....Tigers 7

they will give value for money. Put them against each other and you smell dynamite. I just love their attitude to our game: put the body on the line and never take a backward step.

It didn't take long for them to get into the action and Wakefield's David kicked an early penalty. Soon after, brother Paul was heading for the blood bin after a solid work out with the fists with David Solomona. This fracas unsettled Wakefield who started to get square rather than offer attacking prowess. That played straight into Huddersfield's hands and they slowly started to turn the game around.

Two tries from Sean Penkywicz and Jim Gannon after good work from Jon Grayshon got Wakefield on the back foot and they started to panic, losing possession several times and giving away penalties, although it was a penalty that gave the home side a chance to fight back themselves.

Huddersfield's Julian Bailey went for a spell in the sin-bin and Wakefield took full advantage at a time when the Giants were in command, scoring twice before the break. Solomona and Domic have been outstanding this season and it was those two who put together the move that ended with Domic's try. A mistake by Giants winger Marcus St Hilaire then gave Gareth Ellis the width to put Colum Halpenny over in the corner.

Wakefield coach Shane McNally will have picked up valuable information for the play-offs. He knows his side were sucked into a tough encounter, something they don't need with such class out wide. Lack of concentration at times proved costly, and certainly allowed Darren Fleary, playing his best game this term, to send in Paul White. It took more good work from Jason Demetriou to give Semi Tadulala a try in the corner to bring the scores level. And it was the flying winger who raced 50 metres upfield to gain the position for the Ben Jeffries drop-goal that steered the Wildcats home.

Once again the one-pointer proved vital and sent the fans into raptures, the singing continuing well after we had finished in the studio. We too were happy, seeing as how the last time we were at Wakefield the gantry collapsed!

And collapse is exactly what the St Helens defence did on the same night by throwing away an

18-6 lead against Leeds. All the way through our televised game, the updates from Knowsley Road indicated another humiliation for the Rhinos at the hands of the Saints. Yet again, though, Tony Smith's boys dug deep in the second half to snare a great victory - a fact that was not ignored by the bookies who kept Leeds strong favourites.

Don't write off Saints though. They have bounced back from a slump before and are past masters at winning away from home. That will make Wigan slightly nervous as it's more than likely Ian Millward's men will go to the JJB for the first play-off game. Oh yes, news also came through that the RFL has decided to allow Sean Long to play in next Friday's clash with Bradford. Game on!

Widnes on a cold windy day is not the best. Add driving rain and it makes you want to be on Bondi Beach taking in the sunshine. Could Castleford shine as bright? That was the question on their supporters' lips as they came through the Halton Stadium turnstiles.

Nothing but a win would keep them alive. For Widnes, a draw would do the job. Tense? You bet.

Tigers coach Gary Mercer had not given up hope despite last week's painful loss to Salford

Nervous times at the Halton Community Stadium

and he promised that his squad were prepared to put their bodies on the line. That they did. Mind you, so did Stuart Spruce's charges in a titanic clash that produced such atmosphere one thought there were 100,000 fans shouting their heads off.

Value for money is what we northern folk enjoy most and no refunds were demanded for this epic. Forget about the skill factor, the nerves and weather put paid to that. This was purely and simply about survival, with hearts pounding, adrenalin charging through the body, emotion you could scrape off the walls and fans walking into the ground looking for all the world like they were attending a funeral. It reminded me of Bill Shankly's famous quote about football not being life or death: "it's a lot more important than that." The way these two sides went at each other it certainly appeared that way.

Despite all their possession, Widnes could only score once in the first half but went in at the break looking confident. This was never going to be a high-scoring encounter with the ball sliding all over the place. Having said that, though, the standard of ball control was amazing. We all knew it would be a mistake that turned the game and it came when Brad Davis and Damian Gibson missed a Stephen Myler kick towards the posts. That allowed the kicker to dive over for a converted try.

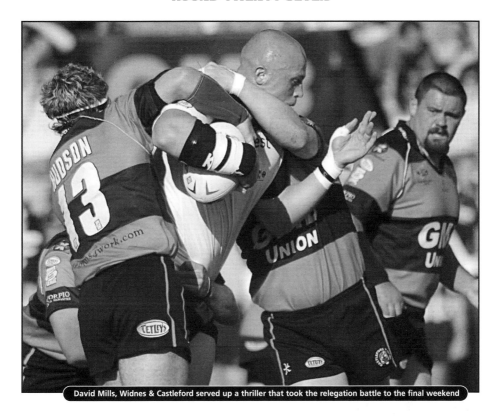

David Mills, Widnes & Castleford served up a thriller that took the relegation battle to the final weekend

Eddie and I intimated at half-time that it would be the biggest pep talk of Mercer's career and so it proved, with some confident play and strong defence on the resumption. Time and time again Castleford got back to stop what looked like a certain try, first Paul Mellor on Deon Bird, then Davis on Pat Devlin, either one would have sealed the victory.

After continually being denied, Widnes were getting frustrated and began looking for the drop-goal. Myler attempted one midway through the second half but watched in agony as it hit the post and bounced out. The miss turned the game again as the Vikings looked dejected.

Castleford must have sniffed that the Gods were on their side and not long after Craig Greenhill made a half-burst before sending sub Jon Hepworth sliding in under the sticks. Godwin's conversion levelled the scores, leaving both sets of fans and players on edge.

Then with ten minutes remaining, enter Mr Francis Maloney with a superb drop-goal from 35 metres. It was sheer class. Cool as a cucumber, the journeyman player set himself and aimed for the target right in front of his following fans, who collectively helped suck the ball over the crossbar. Despite a frenetic finish, that proved just enough to allow the Tigers and Widnes one last throw of the dice next week.

"I can't wait," was the chief thought in my head as I tried desperately to get into my car. Like the Hertz man said: "This will turn a few heads." He's probably right but it's next Saturday that will really catch the eye.

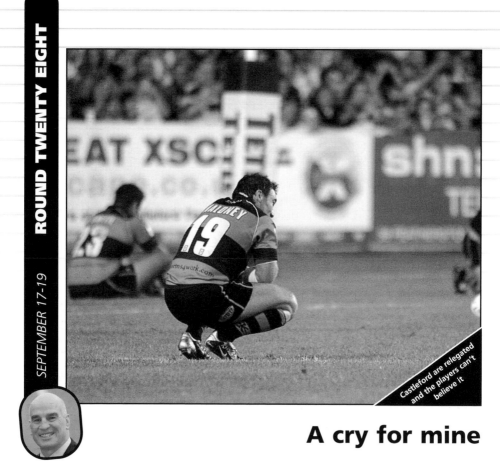

Castleford are relegated and the players can't believe it

A cry for mine

I DIDN'T wear black but I felt like I should because round 28 would spell doom and gloom at either Widnes or Castleford.

Plenty of fans came up to me and suggested who would win or lose as I sped through the country on the train from London to Leeds. That indicated to me that only in times of strife do we unearth fans who probably have never been to a league game in years yet pledge their support with so much gusto one wonders why we don't see over 15,000 at every match.

It dawned on me that it's not just success that brings out the fair weather fan. Oh no, the struggle for survival unearths plenty too and I felt like a traffic accident watching the cars go by.

Thankfully, the 'wake' would have to wait. The return of Sean Long grabbed all the headlines and Bradford, who had expected the cheeky Saint to play anyway, were more than happy to accommodate the "sinner" at the stadium where his betting problems began. I often wonder why fans "boo" players or even myself come to think of it. Is it hate or a weird respect? One thing was for sure, Mr Long was going to get the treatment each time he touched the ball. That didn't stop him from playing out of his skin at a time when he could have been trying to hide under it.

Again, St Helens had players out injured so Bradford were odds on to win on the night. The Bulls were given an extra bonus with the news the team coach

Stevo's Hero!

Lesley Vainikolo.
The Volcano ended the season as he began it - with a record-breaking hat-trick!

Stevo's Zero!

Russell Smith was the latest referee to find himself publicly slammed by Salford coach Karl Harrison

Stevo's pearl

"We will sit down on Monday and decide where we go from here" - Castleford CEO Richard Wright. NL One, Richard!

Rd 28 results

Bulls 64 ....Saints 24
Tigers 28 ......Wildcats 32
Giants 28 ....City Reds 22
Hull 20 ....Vikings 18
Rhinos 42 ......Broncos 14
Warriors 21 ....Wolves 16

from Saints was stuck on the M62 (surprise, surprise) leaving them barely 40 minutes to change and prepare for the fray.

Despite Long's three-month lay-off, he produced some exciting stuff and looked eager and fit, a fact that wouldn't have gone un-noticed by Brian Noble the Great Britain coach. Even so, this wasn't going to be the pony-tailed half-back's day of glory, that went to Lesley Vainikolo who scored his fifth hat-trick of the season to pip Danny McGuire as the Super League's leading try scorer.

Mind you, the Volcano can thank Shontayne Hape for the record. The Kiwi centre turned down a chance to score his own third try of the game by turning away from the posts to look for big Lesley out on the wing. That was a gift four pointer and Stuart Reardon grabbed three tries himself to help Bradford run out easy winners 64-24 and secure that important second spot in the table. They now face Leeds at Headingley in two weeks time in what should be a fantastic contest.

Apart from a mid first-half recovery by Saints, this match

The Widnes Vikings season has a happy ending

was purely about how many points Bradford would score. Yet Ian Millward would have been impressed with his charges for scoring 24 points themselves and the performances, in particular, of youngsters James Roby and Andy Bracek.

Brian Noble was a happy man. He had all but given up on snatching second spot when Hull looked unlikely to be caught, unitl their late-season slump gave the Bulls the green light. So he should be happy after seeing his side play some intelligent, fast-running football with Iestyn Harris and Paul Deacon combining well to ensure the threequarters got plenty of chances. Leon Pryce, too, showed real class for the FULL game and not just the odd minute or two he is inclined to produce.

Not that I needed an excuse, but I toasted Long's return with a glass (or two) of wine that evening in the company of Jimmy Lowes, who had been given the night off to attend one of his testimonial functions. Jimmy looks fitter than when he played! I loosened the belt and consoled my ever-increasing body with a night cap. I needed it too. Nobody sleeps well worrying and I felt for those players who, the following day, would discover their fate one way or the other.

Widnes went to Hull with memories of the 70-4 thrashing behind them and replaced with the knowledge that the men from the KC stadium had hit the brick wall and lost star players like Richard Horne, Paul Cooke, Jason Smith and Paul King. The rejuvenated Vikings felt that they had a good chance of condemning Castleford to the drop and that they did, seeing as how Sky Sports had arranged for all the try-scoring action from the Jungle to be shown on the big screen. Talk about tension. Fans, players and commentators alike were riveted at the twists.

Widnes looked eager and took control for the first quarter of an hour only to see a Stephen Myler charge down produce a Richard Whiting try for Hull against the run of play. Worse still, the split screen showed that Castleford had taken the lead against Wakefield at the Jungle and the groans from the Widnes followers were loud and clear.

TETLEY'S SUPER LEAGUE FINAL TABLE 2004

	P	W	D	L	Diff	PTS
Rhinos	28	24	2	2	594	50
Bulls	28	20	1	7	353	41
Hull FC	28	19	2	7	365	40
Warriors	28	17	4	7	178	38
Saints	28	17	1	10	159	35
Wildcats	28	15	0	13	126	30
Giants	28	12	0	16	-239	24
Wolves	28	10	1	17	-15	21
City Reds	28	8	0	20	-321	16
Broncos	28	7	1	20	-407	15
Vikings	28	7	0	21	-384	14
Tigers	28	6	0	22	-409	12

Full credit to the Vikings, they dug deep to stay in the game and were awarded a rare penalty try when Daniel Frame had the ball stripped away in a two-man tackle as he lunged for the line. Video referee Gerry Kershaw was spot on and it couldn't have come at a better time as Wakefield had just taken the lead as well. It was as though the two games were co-ordinated for, soon after, Castleford scored and then so did Hull from Graeme Horne's high kick when Whiting grabbed his second. Widnes were not to be outdone and Shane Millard sent winger Matt Whitaker in at the corner just before half-time. They got an extra boost with the news that Wakefield had levelled the scores 40 miles down the M62. Things were tight and though I have never bitten my fingernails, I felt like starting.

The game see-sawed in the second stanza and when Jules O'Neill's short pass sent sub Sala Fa'alogo over with eight minutes to go you felt Widnes were safe, so much so that O'Neill's conversion attempt took so long because he, like everyone else in the stadium including the referee, was watching yet another try from the Wildcats on the big screen. How's that for value?

Sadly, those followers down at the Jungle didn't get such great value for money and the huge cheer from Widnes fans which greeted the news that Wakefield had won indicated that the Tigers were doomed. When Colin Best scored late on to give Hull the win, it didn't matter one jot. You would have thought the Vikings had won the Grand Final. Weird to say the least.

I couldn't help but wonder what lies ahead for the Tigers. Most of the side will be snapped up by other Super League clubs, a fact confirmed only hours after this game with news that Hull had signed Motu Tony on a two-year contract. With rumours suggesting Andy Lynch would follow suit and that Ryan Hudson and Wayne Godwin were destined for Bradford also circulating, Castleford are in for a rough ride in trying to get back into the big time.

It was a sad day, but that's sport.

Ewan Dowes & Hull were dumped out by the Wildcats

That'll be McRae!

THE business end!

Sudden death and even more anguish for the fans as we set off into the 2004 play-offs. I felt excited at the prospect of underdogs Wakefield proving a few people wrong and beating Hull at the KC stadium.

And what a clash between Wigan and Saints we had in store the next day! All in all, you just knew these would be tense and nervous times for all involved. Despite having won just three games out of their last ten, Saints were confident, especially with their half-back Sean Long having returned the week before against Bradford with a creditable performance. St Helens boss Ian Millward again played mind games by claiming many of his players were struggling to make the kick-off.

Not that it swayed Wigan coach Denis Betts. Either way, the attraction of another grudge match nearly filled the JJB stadium. I have been amazed at Wigan's resilience and their ability to drag themselves arround the field for 80 minutes whilst looking so tired. Saints started sweetly and caught Wigan cold by ripping their hosts apart with some outstanding play. That should have been the basis for victory, yet the intervention of the video ref and a Kris Radlinski tackle ruled otherwise.

It took ages to decide whether the ball had touched a Saints player in an off-side position before young winger Ian Hardman touched down for what he thought was an 11th-minute try. Yet Wigan got the rub of the green and video ref Steve Cross turned the effort down.

Stevo's Hero!

Wigan full-back Kris Radlinski's last-gasp tackle on Saints' Mickey Higham will be remembered forever

Stevo's Zero!

Leeds' ticket office sold around 11,000 fans Friday night tickets when their clash with Bradford was to be on Saturday

Stevo's pearl

"We made the decision to play the game in our own half" - Wigan coach Denis Betts.

Elimination play-offs results

Hull 18 ....Wildcats 28
Warriors 18 ......Saints 12

Despite that setback, Saints charged on and produced a great burst down the left hand side to give Mickey Higham a golden chance to score under the posts, only for Radlinski to pull off the tackle of the year. Not only did he bring him down short of the posts, he also dislodged the ball from the hooker's grasp.

It was the turning point of the game and Wigan knew it as they quickly regrouped, slowed things down and then set about showing some skills themselves. Once again, Andy Farrell lifted the side and his class provided the chances for Wigan to score twice just before half-time.

Saints looked shocked and never recovered in the second half. The Warriors marched on and left Ian Millward a stunned man. "I thought we were the better side but they took their chances where we frittered away so many," he moaned. It was a great performance from Wigan and hats off to Betts who gets the most out of his side week in week out.

I was left with plenty of time to ponder whether the Warriors could do a repeat of last season and go all the way to the Grand Final whilst trying my best to drive away from the Wigan ground. The JJB is a magnificent stadium, shame about the gridlock it provides after each game - I clocked it at 46 minutes from the ground to Wigan Pier! That's a journey you can walk in 10 minutes or even less if you are fitter than yours truly.

It also had its advantages, though, as fans walked past the car waving and cheering with delight at yet another win over their number one rivals. I just love the League fans. They gleefully walk amongst each other, proudly wearing their team's colours with not a hint of violence. Mind you, one Saints fan did suggest I never knew my father. It's all in good fun and he said it with a huge grin on his face.

Anyway, the season is over for Saints and they can now join the losers of the previous night's game on Humberside, in planning for Super League X.

And what a game that was. Could Wakefield really pull off a shock win at Hull, we all asked, with many of us thinking that, yes, they could. The Wildcats were buoyed, of course, by the fact that Hull had hit the brick wall. They were there for the taking, especially with Paul King and Richard Horne out for the season. That was a blow to club and country but a green light for Wakefield.

Shane McNally has done a great job in dragging Wakefield out of the relegation battle and into the top flight and this was the night when he came to show his side were not just making up the numbers.

Hull started strong, showing much more spirit than in previous weeks and a real battle took place with some crunch tackles that nearly curled Eddie's hair. Boy, this was tough and Wakefield looked a little bemused. It was no shock that Hull went in ahead at half-time and looking confident that they could blow away the visitors.

It amazes me how the half-time break can turn a game around. It happens so often and Wakefield knew they had to lift their standards. Having said that, they were just a few points adrift and would have been happy considering they had two men sent to the sin-bin in that first half. The Wildcats' ploy of messing about at the

Shaun McRae will be a big loss for Hull & Super League

play-the-ball and trying to slow things down upset the referee enough for David Solomona and Gareth Ellis to have to sit out ten minutes in the bin. At one time, Wakefield spent two minutes with only 11 men on the field.

Straight from the restart, though, Wakefield got that touch of inspiration to get the adrenalin pumping. Michael Korkidas, their huge prop, carted the ball upfield 50-odd metres brushing aside no less than six Hull players in the process. That left Hull bewildered and really turned the tide as Wakefield found their class and went on to win.

Hull just fell apart and looked out on their feet, which was a poor way to send off their coach Shaun McRae.

By the time McRae had started his lap of the field to say goodbye to the fans, many black and white shirts had disappeared out into the damp night air. It was a moving sight. McRae has done a wonderful job in his four years at the club. He brought them back from being a disaster side to title contenders. Finishing third in the table is no mean feat and the youngsters at the club will learn from this year's experience. Not surprisingly, Shaun has been invited to no less than 15 farewell functions - a feat only Frank Sinatra could match.

All things come to an end and I even invited the Hull coach for a quiet drink at my hotel well after the game. Thankfully, he accepted for he has become a close friend during his nine years in Britain. So much so that I paid for all the drinks!

Emotion can have a bad effect on your brain cells at times.

The big man will be sadly missed, especially by me. He is the only guest on Sky Sports' Super League coverage that makes me look slim.

Gareth Ellis had little to celebrate at the JJB Stadium

Wildcats so near yet so far

THE Giant killers crossed the Pennines with more than just hope after their second-half showing last week at Hull.

Wigan would start favourites but would not take Wakefield lightly, although most of the Cherry and Whites' fans expected Denis Betts and his boys to do the trick. They were given a huge fright then by the Wildcats' wonderful start, where they ripped Wigan's defence to shreds with ease.

To say the crowd was stunned is an understatement. Wakefield raced to a 14-0 lead within 17 minutes through tries to Colum Halpenny, Duncan Macgillivray and David Solomona. They could have been even further in front if David March had put his kicking boots on. Sadly, he kicked just one conversion and even battling against such a huge margin Wigan still had a glimmer of hope. Time was on their side.

Yet again, it took some magic from Kris Radlinski to get his side out of jail. The full-back somehow got the arm free to score in the corner with four Wakefield players forcing him towards the corner flag after 21 minutes. The home fans breathed an even bigger sigh of relief when Kevin Brown crossed from a Terry Newton pass three minutes later.

A scoreline of 14-10 at half-time hardly showed Wakefield's dominance. They were by far the better side in that first stanza, yet in sudden-death football you take your chances or else! Wigan did just that, scoring twice from only three breaks.

Wakefield, on the other hand, failed to score again as Wigan slowly turned

Stevo's Hero!

Bradford's Paul Deacon was man of the match as the Bulls stunned Headingley by marching straight to Old Trafford

Stevo's Zero!

Video ref Geoff Berry ruled out a good try to Ben Jeffries that could have seen Wakefield's fairytale continue

Stevo's pearl

"I've been glummer. We get to live another day" - Leeds coach Tony Smith looks on the bright side

Qualifying semi-final

Rhinos 12 ....Bulls 26

Elimination semi-final

Warriors 18..Wildcats 14

the screw to snatch the win. It was a sad night for many Wildcats fans who failed to get into the ground before kick-off as there were only two turnstiles open at the visitors end.

That was something which incensed Wakefield MP David Hinchliffe, so much so he slammed the JJB stadium officials. "We all missed the first try and some the second try," he said. "To have only two gates open is totally bizarre. If it had been soccer supporters there would have been a riot."

More controversy was to come when video referee Geoff Berry turned down what appeared to be a perfectly good try from Ben Jeffries in the 59th minute when Wakefield were leading 14-12.

Sid Domic looked as though he had released the ball backwards in the tackle only for Andy Farrell to touch it with his hand. That enabled Semi Tadulala to swoop and put Jeffries away under the posts. To disallow it was a cruel blow, especially as it came at a time when David Solomona was in the sin-bin.

Solomona's sin-binning in itself was a farce. Russell Smith only added to a poor second-half showing by sending the big forward off when it was obvious Radlinski's run had not been stopped.

Again, officials were at the centre of controversy and it proved a fatal blow to Wakefield's chances. Adrian Lam's try with ten minutes to go put Wigan in front for the first time in the match as the visitors continued to throw everything at the Wigan line only to be denied by some wonderful last-ditch defence.

Wigan hung on but coach Denis Betts was far from impressed. "We showed great spirit but we must improve now to get to Old Trafford," was his assessment. He was right, Wigan had dropped far too much ball at crucial moments and it was a relieved Andy Farrell who left the field with his charges.

So, yet another long wait in the car before getting back into Yorkshire. It wasn't just the turnstile fiasco that irritated those who attended the match. Losing is bad enough but to rub mud in your face by making you then wait nearly a whole hour to leave the stadium car park is another slap in the mush. Great stadium, shocking position. One road in, one road out. Result, chaos.

And so to the battle of the big guns, Leeds and Bradford. Yet another page in the history of Super

League classics. A full house yet again and all were expecting a thriller similar to the previous night's Wigan-Wakefield extravaganza.

The atmosphere at Headingley was amazing. Even the sun came out. We had perfect conditions for fast open play of which we got a lot. Only from Bradford, though, who produced great tactics by spurning their normal bash-barge attack down the middle and replacing it with the clever link play that enabled Shontayne Hape to cross twice in the space of 14 minutes. Leeds just weren't at the races and looked shaky, fumbled, stumbled and missed tackles aplenty.

Rhinos boss Tony Smith hasn't shown any emotion before the TV cameras all season yet even he couldn't hide his frustration as his team looked anything but League Leaders. So it took something special to get back into the match and the Leeds player of the year, Matt Diskin, provided it. The hooker booted through a neat grubber which Danny McGuire snapped up to give the South Stand brigade some hope. With Leeds forcing two line drop-outs before the break, Bradford looked wobbly. Even though the Rhinos couldn't snare the points, they would have gone into the sheds in a far more positive frame of mind than could be expected after such a dismal start.

Sadly, injuries to Andrew Dunemann, Kevin Sinfield and Rob Burrow did little to help their cause and, not surprisingly, when Robbie Paul scored only seconds after returning from the bench one felt Bradford were taking control. Jamie Peacock led the way in great fashion, providing the field position for Lee

Stuart Fielden monsters Marcus Bai as Leeds crash to defeat

Radford to cross barely two minutes after Paul's try.

The Rhinos were stunned, although Willie Poching got one back to offer some hope. At 12-20, though, you felt it needed a great fightback to stop Bradford from winning a fourth trip to Old Trafford on the trot. Far too many mistakes and a tendency to off-load in panic proved Leeds downfall and it was pure icing on the cake time when Lesley Vainikolo scored in the final minute from a scrum-base move.

Statistics showed Leeds made 19 clean breaks against Bradford's nine, which should raise their spirits. At least the Rhinos know they have the firepower to crack open defences. Mind you, playing at a tango pace is one thing when a soft shoe shuffle may have proved more beneficial.

Tony Smith's men live on, of course. But they knew it would be Wigan again in their way as they strove to reach the Grand Final. That was a point not lost on one Rhinos fan who disgruntledly left the stadium facing yet another false dawn.

He shouted to me: "All we've won is a silver hub cap! For finishing top of the table! That's not good enough!" And, you know, he's right.

Heather Small sings & the Rhinos get a little excited over Danny McGuire's Championship winning try

keeping calm and ignoring the rumours. Focus, I think, is the word and it was on show to the world when they both appeared on our special Grand Final preview the Friday night before the match. Neither was going to give anything away regarding tactics and you soon realised that both were confident. Brian appeared relaxed and smiling while Tony gave his best impression of a cardboard cut-out. In fact, I felt he would fall asleep at one point. Still, it was great to have them in the studio and where can you find another sport that could bring together the bosses of two big-match clubs only hours before kick-off?

Neville Smith, our boss at Sky, invited the crew to a dinner at a Mexican restaurant after the build-up show and I felt the effects all through the night and early morning. I would have run Speedy Gonzales into second spot in a 100-metre dash. Thankfully, things had settled by the time I set off for the Theatre of Dreams, passing hundreds of fans who were at the ground around 1.00pm in good cheer and voice.

Even commentators get excited at these big games and I couldn't wait to climb the stairs to the gantry to get things under way. Shaun McRae and Andy Farrell were our studio guests, while Adrian Morley was alongside Phil Clarke and Bill Arthur on the touchline, a dream team all of its own.

Former Hull coach McRae was looking forward to having his last farewell (his 64th!) before flying off to Oz and Heather Small got the crowd in a good mood with her magical singing. Not even Heather's great voice could match the noise when the two sides walked out, though. It set the hairs on the back of your head on end. I had to take Eddie's word for that, seeing as how I lost all feeling in that department many years ago. Instead, I polished the dome, took a deep breath and eagerly awaited the kick-off.

I was surprised that when Leeds won the toss they elected to choose ends and not kick-off, a move that would put pressure on the Rhinos defence straight away, as Bradford showed when they took Leeds apart early in their clash two weeks before.

When Kevin Sinfield kicked early in the tackle count, though, it became clear that they were targeting big Lesley Vainikolo. They kicked the ball to him not once, not twice, more like 100 times and the tactic paid off handsomely. You could see the Kiwi winger getting tired as the game wore on.

Most expected the game of the century because of the talent on display but Grand Finals and Cup Finals are not usually like that. Defence is the key and not many clean breaks were on

Leeds hooker Matt Diskin collects the Harry Sunderland Award

display. Even so, it was an arm wrestle of the highest calibre. Despite having to cart the ball back upfield so often, Vainikolo slid in at the corner to give Bradford a lead that lasted until Matt Diskin threw a lovely dummy and glided under the posts. This was going to be one tough encounter as both sides hit each other with such force it looked cruel.

The slippery surface didn't help either, so it was full credit to both sides for the good skills on display. One of those produced what looked to be a great try for Shontayne Hape but the video referee's decision went against the Bulls. The "No Try" call was correct, though, with Lee Radford's off-load coming seconds after the tackle was complete. Anyway, his ball-carrying arm hit the deck and Leeds were off the hook.

The second half was even tighter as defences closed ranks and Vainikolo was left wondering why he yet again had to cart the ball back upfield. The fact that he could hardly get to his feet to play the ball with ten minutes to go indicated that the Smith kick and chase ploy had left the Volcano without much lava.

Bradford again scored early though, when Hape - who has had a fine season - crossed to take the Bulls to within two points of their greatest rivals. But the eager Rhinos snuffed out nearly all their advances, with just a Paul Deacon break to lift their spirits. Sadly, for the Bulls fans, the Leeds defence got back in numbers.

Sport can be cruel and so it proved for poor Robbie Paul, who dropped the ball with no pressure upon him to give Leeds the possession to kill off the game. Who else but Danny McGuire should be there to seal the win, his runaround with Keith Senior creating the space for him to sneak over. Bradford continued to try to get their weary legs working but by then it was all over. Leeds had hung on for victory. No doubt, in the years to come, fans will remember this Grand Final for Paul's dropped ball.

Yes, it was a mistake but it would be harsh to suggest that was the only reason Leeds won. In fact, it would be an insult to the Rhinos' effort. Leeds were

just too good, simple as that, although many Rhinos fans will never forget the gloating from the Bulls supporters who poked fun at Kevin Sinfield when he took a quick tap instead of going for goal in the 2003 Challenge Cup Final. That was a decision that allowed Bradford to pick up the trophy and they even had t-shirts made and posted a huge banner on the Leeds/Bradford border, reminding the young Rhinos skipper of his boo-boo. It was with great pleasure, then, that the same guy's goal-kicking proved the difference this time. I'm sure he had a look of satisfaction and revenge on his face when he lifted the Super League trophy.

Sinfield, Mathers and Diskin all shone brightly throughout the game but it was pleasing to see a hooker at long last pick up the Harry Sunderland award for man of the match. It was the first time that has happened in 31 years and it is fitting that Matt Diskin got the nod. He has had a great year and fully deserved to get into the Great Britain squad for the Gillette Tri-Nations series.

Unfortunately, just a few hours later, Leeds skipper Sinfield would discover that his own efforts had not been good enough to join Diskin, Danny McGuire, Keith Senior, Chev Walker, Danny Ward and Ryan Bailey into the GB camp. Like I said, sport can be cruel at times.

I always feel sad when driving away from Old Trafford. The euphoria is gone, the fans are gone and after a while even the tonnes of litter will be gone. But Shaun McRae? No, he'd not gone. In fact, he asked for a lift back to the hotel where he suggested we have, yes, another farewell!

"Why not?" I replied. "It's just like our game. You can't get enough!" Anyway, 65 is my lucky number.

Leeds
Rhinos

AUTOGRAPHS